Who Killed Patricia Curran?

Kieran Fagan

First published in 2022 by Kieran Fagan, 31 Seafield Court, Killiney, Dublin A96 PH 32, Ireland. Copyright: Kieran Fagan.

ISBN: 978-1-7396719-0-7

In memory of Andy and Maureen Fagan

WHO KILLED PATRICIA CURRAN?

Kieran Fagan was born in Dublin 1945 where he still lives. He worked for newspapers and in public relations for many years and now 'ghost writes' books for clients and publishes under his own name.

By the same author

The Framing of Harry Gleeson

Upstart (with Ed Walsh)

The Story of HB (with Paul Mulhern)

Contents

Who killed Patricia Curran?

– how a vulnerable young man was framed for murdering
Patricia Curran age 19 in Whiteabbey in Northern Ireland
in 1952

Kieran Fagan

*'We plead with everyone who has the slightest piece of
information that might lead the police to trace the murderer
of our dear daughter to give such information to the police.'*

– Doris and Lancelot Curran, 14 November 1952

Preface

I had three main reasons for writing this book.

Iain Hay Gordon's trial in Belfast for the murder of Patricia Curran coincided with an outbreak of measles in Dublin. In 1953 I was just eight years old, home from school, spotty and bored, and reading everything I could lay my hands on. Every day when my father returned from work every day with the *Irish Press*, I devoured the court reports, culminating with a lengthy account of the final day and the verdict.

It would be good to say that I smelt a rat from the beginning, but it wouldn't be true. I did become suspicious when I began to read Eoin McNamee's The Blue Tango in 2000. It was, according to acclaimed critic Eileen Battersby, reviewing it for *The Irish Times*, 'the finest Irish novel for many years'.

I agree that the writing is fluent and accomplished. However it is also a ghastly travesty of the truth and my second reason for addressing this subject. McNamee's 'novel' – note that word – distorted the record in naming real people and the places they lived in. Patricia Curran's murder is in the recent and painful past. On the cover of the paperback edition of 2002 is a slightly blurred but recognisable image of Patricia. It cannot be right to play with facts and destroy the reputations of those who cannot rebut his cruel fictions.

Patricia Curran was a likeable, pleasant and practical-minded young woman when she was stabbed 37 times and died a dreadful death. According to the autopsy report, she was a virgin. Not in McNamee's telling. On page five his characters tell us that ' she had been involved with three married men in the previous year'. Turn over the page and she's having sex with a man she didn't know 'wearing her school uniform'. 'He remembered how cold the metal clasp of her bra strap had felt in his hand'.

Later, on page 195, McNamee repeats the accusation. 'In the evening the men walked to the bars. They talked about Patricia Curran. Rumours had reached them about her sexual history. They said she drank in the bars of Amelia Street, where the whores were. She was the kind of girl that was referred to as being out of control. They thought she might be better off as a victim of murder. It brought a softness to her. Her hard little body, her hard little face. That feeling of an untimely end. They felt it had rescued her femininity.'

I felt sick when I first read that passage. I still do.

My third reason for this book is that I wanted to find out all I could about what happened to the real Patricia Curran and the other principal victim of this tragedy, the young Scottish airman Iain Hay Gordon. I wanted to dig out the truth beneath the lies and sly innuendoes. This story has victims and villains and decent men and women too. In particular I invite readers to witness the goodness of Dorothy Turtle and her band of supporters, some of whom were Quakers, but not all.

I hope you will get something useful from reading it.

Kieran Fagan, 1 May 2022, Dublin .

WHITEABBEY

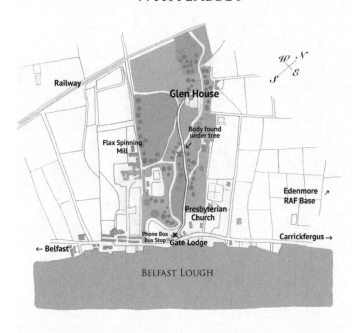

Figure 1: The village of Whiteabbey, Co Antrim. lies on the northern shore of Belfast Lough on the road to Carrickfergus. Patricia Curran got off the bus in the village at the phone box and went north up the avenue to her home Glen House. The black X shows where she began walking up the avenue, and the red X where her body was found. Copyright Fiona Aryan.

CHAPTER 1

Whiteabbey, Co Antrim in the 1950s

History and geography meet in the glistening waters of Belfast Lough. As you travel north through County Antrim, you became aware that Scotland is not far away, neither physically nor culturally. The main strands of this story come together in Whiteabbey, a pleasant village on the shores of the lough, about five miles north of Belfast. Shore Road runs north eastwards from Belfast along the edge of the lough; at times it becomes the A2 road and the M2 motorway. A striking white Victorian church dominates the skyline. At the time in which the events described this book happened, there were houses and shops on both sides of Whiteabbey's main street, including Archie McFaul's coal yard and three public houses. Today it looks very different. Shore Road continues to follow the edge of the lough; but the waterside buildings have gone. The main street has swerved inland. In effect, while retaining some landmarks and familiar shape, Whiteabbey 'jumped' sideways and inland. Another prominent feature then was an electric-powered double-sided clock on a bracket, protruding from the upstairs of an end of terrace house, known to locals as 'Clock Corner', where older men would congregate for a yarn and a laugh.

Close to a bridge over the river, known as Three Mile Water, Johnston Star flute band's practice hall stood beside where the present-day Glenville Road joins Shore Road.

Being so close to Belfast, and having views across the lough, made the townland of White Abbey and its surroundings sought-after places to live for those with money to spend. Confusingly the townland name has two words, while the village, Whiteabbey has just one.

When the Curran family moved into Glen House in 1944, from a house called Benvista in nearby Jordanstown, the weaving factory hooter used to summon workers, and the fields were still used for bleaching flax. But the linen industry was in decline, and the village of Whiteabbey was on the way to becoming a comfortable Belfast suburb, home to many of the unionist aristocracy who dominated the business and political life of Northern Ireland. A declining number of people still worked in the mills, but those jobs would vanish in the decade to come.

Patricia Curran played her own small part in the changes that were happening in her home place. In 1951, after leaving Richmond Lodge School in Armagh where she was a boarder, she had taken on a holiday job driving for a firm called Mapco. A slim but sturdy young woman, she made deliveries to a nearby site at Rathcoole, where intense building activity was in the process of making it the largest housing project for its time on the island of Ireland. There she helped the surveyor to mark out the lines for the foundations of the new buildings with his stakes and balls of twine. She delivered plumbing items, sinks and toilet bowls from her employer's van on to the site. Patricia Curran must have enjoyed this work because she took a year out from July 1951 to August 1952 before beginning her studies at Queen's University, Belfast in September 1952, with a view to becoming a hospital almoner. Today a young woman like her would probably choose to study engineering or science.

At the village of Whiteabbey, behind the landmark Presbyterian church, lay a verdant glen with a stream running through it. The private avenue leading to Patricia Curran's home was on Shore Road, at right angles to the lough. A pillared gateway and a gate lodge gave access to a drive. After about 200 yards the drive forked, the left-hand avenue continuing through the trees up to Glen House, the right fork leading to Glenavna and its demesne, home to Sir Wilson Hungerford.

Here the land rises steadily from the lough shore, and at the top stand imposing railway viaducts, sometimes called the 'Bleach Green' viaducts. The shimmering watercourse of the Three Mile Water meanders through the grounds of the big houses into Belfast Lough, and the winding driveway up to Glen House crosses it. The area was known to locals as the 'Valley of Death' because of the dramatic scale of the viaducts. Freeman Wills Crofts, a celebrated author of detective fiction, designed the viaducts in his earlier career as a civil engineer. Another viaduct nearby features in a handsome 1930s' travel poster, *Greenisland Viaducts*, designed by Sir Norman Wilkinson R.A., though the title is misleading, Greenisland being a couple of miles away.

The big houses facing the lough were built as homes for Victorians, many of whom had distinguished themselves in various walks of life. Anthony Trollope's fourth novel, *The Warden*, published in 1855, was written at Whiteabbey, while he was living in a house there called 'Fernagh'. The architect and railway engineer Robert Young lived at a house called 'Abbeyville', and James Bryce, lawyer, historian and politician who was British ambassador to the United States from 1907 to 1913, spent his formative years living with his grandfather at the same address.

At a nearby house called 'Rathfern', Sir Walter Campbell grew up. He served as deputy quartermaster general to the Mediterranean expeditionary force and took part in the evacuation from Gallipoli in January 1916. He was a brother of Ulster Unionist MP Lloyd Campbell, who lived at Glen House before the Curran family. Later, just a year before Patricia Curran was murdered, Lady Henrietta Staples, a member of the distinguished Anglo-Irish Ussher family, married and moved into a 'cottage' at Whiteabbey and spent the next quarter century living there. Her father, the writer Arland Ussher, was a close friend of Samuel Beckett.

Sir Crawford McCullagh (1868-1948) was lord mayor of Belfast during both world wars and is credited with much of the city's commercial success. As an impoverished young man, he liked to walk out to Whiteabbey from Belfast on Sundays with his young wife Minnie. The couple dreamt 'of living in in one of the grand houses built on the shores of Belfast Lough with their well-manicured lawns hidden behind high hedges and ornate wrought iron railings.'[i] He had married Mary (Minnie) McCully in 1890, but she died of TB, and it wasn't until much later that McCullagh and his second wife, Maggie, moved into their splendid residence 'Lismara' in Whiteabbey in 1915.

By that time Maggie Brodie had become Lady Margaret McCullagh, chatelaine of a fine Italianate sandstone residence on nineteen acres, and she and her husband joined the congregation of Whiteabbey Presbyterian church, where Patricia Curran's brother Desmond would later meet Iain Hay Gordon. There was another connection. McCullagh's daughter Helen was a keen horsewoman and gave riding lessons to Patricia.

The Curran family moved into Glen House for political reasons in 1944. Lancelot Curran, known as Lance, was the member of the parliament at Stormont for the Carrick division, as it was called, and needed to live in his constituency. Lance and his wife Doris (Dorrie) had previously lived in nearby Jordanstown. Glen House – sometimes referred to as The Glen but that name really belongs to the sloping woodland in which it is situated – had been built for John Shelley, a customs official, in 1863. Photographs of the house do not do justice to its size, nor the scale of its presence among the trees surrounding it. Built into a sloping site, the living rooms are at ground floor level at the front, and some first-floor windows at the back are also at ground level. At Glen House, this unusual layout had implications for the tragedy to come.

Glen House was surrounded by magnificent woodland. The trees were planted in the early to mid-nineteenth century and by the time Lance Curran moved in would have included sequoias, Lebanese cedars and magnificent redwoods. Unlike other large houses in the district, Glen House did not have a view of Belfast Lough. Instead it had a spectacular woodland setting. Today, Glenavna still exists but Glen House burned down in a fire in 1988.

Retired solicitor and former member of parliament Stratton Mills recalled visiting the Curran home at the invitation of Desmond Curran whom he came to know as a student in Queen's University. 'The judge was very much the host, even though Desmond had invited me. He spoke very openly to me, despite the fact that I was only a first-year law student', Mills says. 'At that stage, Lance Curran already been a Stormont MP and Northern Ireland's youngest attorney general and had become a high court judge. He spoke freely about the fact that he had become a judge too early. He said he should have stayed longer at the Bar and made some money.'

The subject of judge's pay was of more than passing interest to Stratton Mills. His own father was a judge, being resident magistrate for the county of Antrim. When the RUC eventually charged Iain Hay Gordon with the murder of Patricia Curran, it was Dr J.V.S. (Victor) Mills, who remanded him in custody and later conducted the depositions hearings which preceded Gordon's trial for murder.

Lance Curran's elder son Desmond was an important figure in the law faculty at Queen's University in 1950 when Stratton Mills studied there. Desmond had previously won a scholarship to Trinity Hall, Cambridge; there he studied classics. In Cambridge, Desmond shared rooms with another student from Northern Ireland, John McDermott, a son of Lord Chief Justice John Clarke McDermott, the judge who would pass sentence on Iain Hay Gordon for Patricia Curran's murder. At Queen's, Desmond had been chairman of the law students' society, a position that boded well for a glittering legal career. But Desmond had another passion and he wanted to sign up the young Stratton Mills for it. Moral Re-Armament[ii] was a cause taken up by many young people after the horrors of World War I and in the growing realisation that another was coming. At a meeting of 3,000 in East Ham Town Hall, London, on 29 May 1938, Protestant evangelist Frank Buchman, an American, launched a campaign for Moral Re-Armament. 'The crisis is fundamentally a moral one,' he said. 'The nations must re-arm morally. Moral recovery is essentially the forerunner of economic recovery. Moral recovery creates not crisis but confidence and unity in every phase of life.'

Today the language seems oddly militaristic. Yet Moral Re-Armament had become a powerful force in a century sickened by wars. With its emphasis on personal responsibility and deepening the spirituality of its members, drawn from various Christian groups, it had a special appeal for young people like Desmond Curran, looking for a guiding light to live by, something with greater contemporary relevance than the traditional churches offered. Hitler's Nazi regime took Moral Re-Armament to be a serious threat, imprisoning its leaders and supporters. Some 240 British MPs had sent messages of support to the movement's launch in Washington in 1939. In the United

States Senator Harry Truman campaigned for Moral Re-Armament. After World War II, influential European leaders including German Chancellor Konrad Adenauer and French Foreign Minister Robert Schumann gave it their support.

In Belfast Desmond Curran proselytised for the cause, seeking new recruits among his friends and acquaintances, including an oddball Scottish national serviceman Iain Hay Gordon who was posted to the RAF barracks at Edenmore, which was within easy walking distance of the Curran home at Whiteabbey. Another target was a RUC sergeant, Samuel Deveney. He had shown some interest when Desmond Curran raised the subject with him. Michael Curran, Desmond's younger brother, poured scorn on Moral Re-Armament, and made it clear that he wanted nothing to do with it, and told his brother in front of family and friends that he was wasting his time.

Edenmore, where Gordon was sent to do his national service, had been built for James Torrens (1796-1884), a wealthy solicitor and land agent for the Donegall and Shaftesbury Irish estates. The house and demesne became RAF Edenmore, an administrative base for No. 67 NI Reserve Group and No 3502 (Ulster) Fighter Control Group. After the RAF left, it became a hotel, then a care home. Today modern apartment blocks have taken its place, with no sign of it ever having been a military base.

Nor does Whiteabbey today give up any secrets, though a village of that name does feature in a recent literary genre known as 'Ulster Noir'. This description was given to a series of well-crafted crime novels by Eoin McNamee, which adopted the names and lives of real people, including Patricia Curran, members of her family and friends, and others. Although the names and the places are real, the account of events is fictitious. Unfortunately, some of the author's fictional flourishes have entered public perceptions of this case, thus gaining the status of 'fact'.

Early on the morning of Thursday 13 November 1952, five or six policemen wearing heavy dark green overcoats scrabbled on hands and knees through wet undergrowth in the woods near Glen House. Some had pushed their caps back on their heads, so the dull badge pointed up at the few stars to be seen when the clouds parted. The men advanced, some crouching, others on their knees, their breath heavy on the night air. They found a fur glove to add to the shoes, two scarves and a cap already recovered between where the young woman's body was found and the avenue up to the house. A sergeant spotted a button, which was added to the trove. Some books were neatly piled one on top of the other by the side of the avenue as if they been carefully placed there. They were not wet though the ground on which they stood was. There was very little blood to be seen considering the victim had been stabbed repeatedly. Where stabbing has occurred, you expect to see blood, increasing in volume as the blows continue. Bits and pieces of a smashed wristwatch were also found in the foliage, suggesting that the woman had raised her arm to fend off the blows. The watch face was missing. It might have revealed exactly when this dreadful assault took place.

The body of a nineteen-year-old female lay about 40 feet in from the avenue leading to her home. She had been subjected to a dreadful battering. The autopsy would conclude that Patricia Curran had been hit one almighty blow, rendering her unconscious or semi-conscious. She had then been stabbed 37 times with a short knife or rapier. Any one of eight of those blows went deep enough to kill her.

Her eldest brother Desmond had found her body in the woods along the avenue that led up to the family home, Glen House, close to the northern shore of Belfast Lough. He, his father and a family friend had placed the body into a car and driven it to the family doctor's house, where the young woman's stiffened limbs immediately indicated that she was dead.

She had been brightly dressed on the November day when she had met her death. Her Juliet cap – some called it a beret – was yellow as were her scarves, one made of wool, the other of silk. They contrasted boldly against the dull brown of her coat. The yellow theme continued in her check skirt, topped with a brown cardigan.

When the phone rang shortly after 1.30 on the morning of November 13, 1952, in the cramped police station on Shore Road which runs through Whiteabbey, two policemen were present. Constable Hutchinson answered the call. 'Yes, Mrs. Curran, yes, yes'. Then he put down the phone and roused his sleeping colleague from his bed. 'There's something wrong at Judge Curran's house. You'd better get up there straightaway' he told Constable Edward Rutherford. Hutchinson reached for his book of phone numbers and set about ringing District Inspector L. Mahaffy, who wouldn't be pleased to be woken up, and less so when he heard what the phone call was about. There was a slight drizzle as Rutherford cycled the short distance along the Shore Road and turned right through the gates of the avenue leading up to Glen House and Glenavna. 'I took a torch with me', Rutherford said. 'I met Judge Curran. I heard shouting. The judge and I ran towards the direction of the shouting. Before we reached the place where the shouting came from, I noticed the lights of a car coming along the avenue. I signalled to the driver to stop. I then went to where the light [Desmond Curran's torch] was in the undergrowth. I found the body of Patricia Curran lying at the foot of a tree. The body was stretched out, with the head towards the river, and the feet towards the avenue. Just then Mr Davison arrived on the scene. The judge, Mr Davison and Desmond Curran lifted the body and carried it to the car.'

According to Desmond Curran, when he had returned home around 9pm, his sister had not returned from university. His parents, Lance Curran and his wife Doris, were present; his younger brother Michael had stayed in Belfast and was not due home that night. When Desmond had gone to bed at about 11pm, Patricia was still not home. At about 1.30am, his mother woke him[1] and said that they needed to find out where she was. He got up and went with his mother to a house on Shore Road to see if there was any news there of his sister. Sometimes if there was no one at home, Patricia went to a neighbour to ask for a lift up the avenue. On the way down the avenue and later going back up, his mother drove the car and Desmond looked out for any sign of Patricia. There was none. Nor did he see the portfolio with her books lying on the side of the avenue where they were later found.

Lance Curran had phoned the Davisons who lived not far away at Greenisland to ask his friend Malcolm, who was also his family solicitor, to come to Glen House as Patricia was missing. Desmond decided to search the grounds of the house and borrowed a torch. He set off down the drive to the first bridge over the stream that runs through the grounds, shining the torch left and right, shouting his sister's name. He then widened his trajectory, zigzagging through the shrubbery on both sides of the avenue.

In the distance he could hear his father calling out Patricia's name. After a while Desmond spotted a body lying under a tree, beside bushes, about 40 feet in from the avenue. He noticed blood and cuts on his sister's face. He dropped the torch and picked her up. 'In raising her body, I heard a sound like breathing.' He called out for help.

His father and Constable Rutherford arrived just as Desmond put down the body. Very shortly lights coming up the drive indicated that Malcolm Davison and his wife Doreen had arrived in their car. Still maintaining that Patricia was alive, Desmond, his father and Malcolm Davison lifted her into the Davison's car. 'I got into the back of the car and the body was across my knees', Desmond said later. Patricia's legs were stiff, and Mrs. Davison tried to push them into the car, but the rear door still wouldn't close. She got into the driving seat, with her husband beside her, and drove with Patricia's feet protruding to the nearby house of the Curran's family doctor Dr. Kenneth Wilson.

As there was no room to turn the car in the avenue, Doreen Davison had to drive up the avenue to Glen House to turn the car. Doris Curran must have heard the car approaching and probably saw it turning in front of the house.

So it was that three sworn officers of the court, a judge and his son, Lance and Desmond Curran, both barristers, and a solicitor, Malcolm Davison, unlawfully disturbed a murder scene, observed and unhindered by another officer of the law, RUC Constable Edward Rutherford.

Also at some stage on the evening of November 12, or the morning of November 13, Lance Curran spoke to Sir Richard Pim, inspector general of the RUC, by telephone about his daughter but when and what was said is not known.

Rutherford went back to the police barracks to report, and a little while later returned to the crime scene with Sergeant William Black and another constable to begin a search of the surrounding area, though it was still dark. There they were joined by Head Constable James Cochrane who made a sketch of the area [head constable was an RUC rank above sergeant but below inspector] District Inspector Mahaffy, and Detective Sergeant Samuel Deveney. Other police came and went as the grounds were searched and evidence gathered. Patricia Curran's body was moved to Belfast where a post-mortem examination was performed by Dr. Albert Wells.

But it was too late – the fault line that has forever dogged the investigation of the murder of Patricia Curran was already in place. Within a few minutes of the discovery of the body, one crime scene where the body lay had been disturbed, and another potential one, the Curran home, where the murder might well have happened, had not been secured. The ordinary procedures of law in dealing with murder were not and would not apply, it transpired, because the victim was a judge's daughter.

The consequences of those initial grave mistakes in the early hours of the morning of 13 November 1952 would include a confession extracted by threat – some say blackmailed – out of a vulnerable young man called Iain Hay Gordon, a botched trial and a wrongful guilty conviction. This began half a century of campaigning against a miscarriage of justice, a change in the law governing appeals, and in 2000 a successful appeal which left the public no nearer knowing who the guilty party was than had been the case almost fifty years ago. Today seventy years have passed since that murder and those consequences have not been resolved. The Royal Ulster Constabulary is no more, but its successor, the Police Service of Northern Ireland, still lists this case as an unsolved murder.

Later that morning in Whiteabbey, news of the murder spread quickly. At Edenmore camp a postman told Iain Gordon – and everyone else he met on his round – that the judge's daughter had been 'shot'. The *Northern Whig,* published in Belfast, got it right the next day: 'Stabbing caused death of Patricia Curran' the headline read.

At Edenmore the Royal Air Force's internal police were quickly out of the traps. But first the non-commissioned officers 'did the rounds' the next day, telling the conscripts at the camp to have their alibis ready: who was with whom, so the civilian police would not be able to pin the matter on a serviceman, as so often happened. However, this was much more serious than a punch-up with locals outside a pub over a pretty girl.. [iii]

Since the reason Gordon came to offer a false alibi would consume hundreds of hours of police and court time, and many thousands of words would be written about it, a significant level of detail is necessary in this present account.

On Thursday 13 November RAF police Sergeant Maxey told the recruits to have their alibis sorted out for the period up to midnight on Wednesday 12 November. The recruits were questioned about their whereabouts during this period. Those questioned included Iain Hay Gordon. He was not a suspect at this stage.

The RUC subsequently informed the military police that the murder probably happened before six pm, soon after Patricia Curran got off the bus at Whiteabbey at 5.20pm. On the Friday military police questioned the men at Edenmore again, this time concentrating on their movements between 5.30pm and 6.30pm.

Neither Leading Aircraftman Iain Hay Gordon nor Corporal Henry Connor had alibis for that period, so mindful of what Sergeant Maxey had told them, they agreed to say that they had been together in the camp canteen at 5pm, then had separated to go their respective billets. This was simply not true. Gordon never had an alibi for that time.

Both Gordon and Connor repeated this lie consistently until 14 January 1953 when Gordon broke assisting the RUC in investigating the murder.

Lawyers and policemen who had done national service and 'knew the score' should have recognised a common practice in the daily life of a military barracks. The men were lying because they had been told to lie. Military orders are orders. That didn't stop a lengthy and wasteful 'wild goose chase' for a complex conspiracy where none existed, though it did justify those policemen who suspected that Gordon was not being completely truthful with them. If he was lying about one thing, couldn't he be lying about others?

But all this lay in the future. On 13 November, an evening newspaper, the *Belfast Telegraph*, brought news of a shocking murder in Whiteabbey. There was interest abroad too. That afternoon the *Aberdeen Evening Express* in the north east of Scotland told its readers: 'Judge's Daughter Found Shot Dead'. The next day the *Belfast Newsletter* reported on the post-mortem results: 'Miss Curran's death was caused by stab wounds which it would appear were inflicted by a sharp instrument, possibly of the stiletto type.'

Readers were told that the victim was a dark-haired first year student in the faculty of arts at Queen's University, Belfast. 'On Wednesday afternoon she played squash in the university drill hall and she left Belfast to return home by bus early in the evening. It was Miss Curran's habit to telephone home for a car to be sent to pick her up at the bus stop at Whiteabbey village. Towards midnight when there had been no communication from her, her family phoned the police, having first telephoned a number of houses where she might have called.'

In fact, Patricia Curran did not play squash that afternoon, though she had planned to, because there was no free court available at Queen's. Instead she had coffee with her friend and fellow student John Steele, after which she also changed her mind about going to the cinema and went home instead.

The *Belfast Newsletter* report of 14 November quoted her brother Michael:

> There is no doubt that my sister came straight home from university on the 5 o'clock bus. It was her custom when she arrived at Whiteabbey village to telephone home and let us know she had arrived, and someone has always gone down to the village and fetched her home. If she found

there was no one at home, there was always one or two people in the village who would bring her home instead. She always, without exception, had taken advantage of one of these alternatives and this was the first time she had not done so.

As the hours went by and she did not give us the customary ring, my father became very worried. I was in Belfast at the time, but my brother Desmond went out to see if he could find her and I joined him when I got home. None of us has the slightest idea of any possible motive for murder – not the slightest idea. There are rabbits in the area and which country people come along and shoot but not in the particular part where my sister was killed.

My sister had been driving a van for an engineering company for some time and she had just left that and gone up to Queen's University where she was an undergraduate training to be an almoner.

A *Northern Whig* report added that Patricia was 'an unassuming, quiet girl, well-liked among the people of the district. She was well-known as an animal lover and had visited horse shows frequently with local breeders.'

Michael Curran is practically invisible in subsequent accounts of his sister's murder, and the *Belfast Newsletter* reporter did well to get him on the record. He was the second of Lance and Doris's children, older than Patricia and younger than Desmond. Like Desmond, Michael had attended King William College, a boarding school in the Isle of Man, but his academic record never reached his brother's heights. The Isle of Man may seem like an odd place to send children to boarding school, but war was raging, and Belfast's shipyards were a magnet for German bombers. Michael then spent a year at Queen's University but left without graduating. As to his movements on the night of the murder, it is clear that he had planned to stay in Belfast but was contacted and told to return home and did so. He does not say at what time Desmond went out to look for Patricia.

An unnamed source at Queen's was quoted, in the *Belfast Newsletter*, saying that Patricia had only recently taken up playing squash. Alexander McDonald, director of physical education at the university, also chimed in to tell reporters that Patricia was a 'well-built, fit young girl' and said she was keen on most games. In fact, she was five feet eight inches tall, of slim build, weighing nine stone, almost exactly the same dimensions as those of the man who would be accused of murdering her.

Newspaper reports also noted the arrival in Belfast of Dr. James Firth, a forensic chemist from the British North-West Forensic Science laboratory at Preston, Lancashire, to help the investigation.

The inquest on Patricia Curran began in the British Legion club in Whiteabbey on the Friday morning. Desmond and Michael Curran attended. After the body had been identified, the coroner, Dr Herbert Baird, adjourned to allow the police inquiries to proceed. Desmond said his sister was fit and well on the morning of 11 November. The next time he had seen her on the morning of 13 November she was dead.

On Saturday 15 November, Lance and Doris Curran's appeal for witnesses, made the previous evening, was published by newspapers:

> We plead with everyone who has the slightest piece of information that might lead the police to trace the murderer of our dear daughter to give such information to the police. There may be some who are in possession of useful information but who not desire to divulge their names. We plead with such people to get in touch with the

police, or us, by anonymous letter or telephone. Our telephone number is Whiteabbey 2103.

We are concerned to see that this foul murderer is brought to justice, not through any spirit of vengeance, but to ensure that other people's daughters may be safe. We keep asking ourselves – who will be the next victim?

Patricia's funeral on Saturday 15 November, was preceded by a short service in the family home, led by Rev. William B. McMurray, a retired minister of Whiteabbey Presbyterian church, because Doris Curran was not well enough to attend her daughter's funeral. The motor hearse then drove slowly through the village of Whiteabbey where every shop was closed, window blinds pulled down and the people of the village – of all denominations – lined the pavements. Lance Curran and his sons walked behind the hearse.

At the family burial plot in Drumbeg churchyard near Lisburn, the incumbent Whiteabbey minister, Rev. Sam Wylie, spoke of the love everyone who knew her had for Patricia Curran: 'The spirit of our Patricia has gone marching gloriously on. The soul of our dear one is the hands of one more tender than any mother, more loving than any father. Winsome in her young womanhood, she held her sure place in all our affection and interest.' Wylie appealed to the murderer to come forward and confess, 'knowing that every extenuating circumstance will be weighed in the sensitive balance of our British law.' An odd time for a clergyman to mention extenuation, one might think.

Over the weekend of the funeral, the police issued a description of a man they wanted to speak to, 'aged about 26 or 27, height 5ft 9 inches, hair light brown with the eyebrows noticeably darker. Medium build, dark eyes, no head dress, said to speak with an educated Northern Ireland accent.'

This description was circulated to laundries and dry-cleaning shops, in case the murder was trying to get rid of bloodstains from his clothes, and also to public transport operators. It probably originated with Mrs Gorman, a tea-shop owner in Carrickfergus, who had responded to the appeal for information by reporting a recent strange customer whom she suspected was sleeping rough.

According to Sir Richard Pim, inspector-general and thus head of the RUC, police shorthand writers were answering telephone calls from the public in response to the Curran parents' appeal for information: 'We particularly want the public to let us know if they saw any strange cars or people in the vicinity of Whiteabbey around 5.20pm. There are motorists known as "kerb crawlers" in and about Belfast, and though Miss Curran was certainly not the kind of girl to have anything to do with them, there were complaints from the Whiteabbey area some time ago, and we are anxious to know if there were any such motorists about on the evening of the murder.'

Sir Richard said that he was not satisfied that Patricia Curran had been murdered at the spot where she was found. The fact that three buttons from her coat were found 30 feet away from her body suggested that she had been lifted and either carried or dragged to where she was found. Yet there were no indications of a struggle., he said. 'I think', Sir Richard said, 'it was all done so quickly she did not have a chance of defending herself.'

Behind the scenes, the RUC was cranking up the largest investigation it had ever undertaken. The police would speak to more than 40,000 people and take statements from approximately 9,000. RUC County Inspector Albert Kennedy, the senior detective for County Antrim including Belfast city, told Sir Richard that he was looking closely at possible suspects, including a troubled young man, Gideon Crawford, aged twenty-five, who lived at Cambrai Park in Whiteabbey, about a mile from the scene of the crime. He had violently attacked people in the past and been a patient at Holywell Hospital, the mental asylum, a number of times, where the medical superintendent, Dr. Gilbert Smith, on seeing photographs of Patricia Curran's wounds suggested that someone with an illness like Crawford's could be responsible. Donald Gilchrist, chief nursing officer at Holywell, who had witnessed Crawford having violent epileptic fits, concurred with his superior's opinion. Crawford was living at home when the murder took place, and he had no alibi, though at first his mother claimed that he had one. In the days after the Curran murder, Crawford's father, who had previously sought the release of his son from custody, had changed tack and been asking to have him readmitted to Holywell.

It was more than a coincidence, Kennedy told Sir Richard Pim, that such a man was living so close to the scene of the crime, and that his parents had been asking for him to be hospitalised. Kennedy's interim conclusion was that the case against Crawford was not strong enough to charge him.

Another line of inquiry came from a report to police by Mrs. Elizabeth Eaton of Fernagh Garden Village, Whiteabbey. She said that she had heard a scream coming from the direction of Glen House just after nine o'clock on the night of 12 November. Another Whiteabbey woman, Mrs Jeanette Sloan, said she heard a chain rattling on the gate shared by Glen House and Glenavna between 5.45 and 5.50pm on the evening of the murder. She said that she heard someone running fast down the road towards Whiteabbey. That could have been the newspaper delivery boy George Chambers who told police he had been frightened by a sudden noise in the avenue leading up to Glen House and so had ran away. That was on Wednesday 12 November.

But more intriguing information came from a schoolgirl who lived in Whiteabbey and had known Patricia

Curran since early childhood. Marcella Devlin, aged twelve, had been in the avenue leading to the Curran's house about a month earlier when she saw a Hillman car driving up. Patricia Curran got out of it and walked up towards her front door. The driver had a scar on the left side of his face running from the corner of his mouth to his eye.

Marcella Devlin was an observant girl and she noticed that the car's front and rear registration plates bore different numbers. She saw the same man the next day in the avenue leading to Glen House. On foot this time, he intercepted Patricia, spoke sharply to her and she ran away towards her home. Marcella Devlin saw the man a final time in late October. Patricia was walking in front of her, and the man emerged from a gateway on Shore Road and spoke to her. Patricia looked frightened. When the man saw Marcella, he cleared off.

At first the RUC was disinclined to believe this account, but the head nun at the Dominican College in Belfast vouched for Marcella Devlin. She was a very intelligent and advanced student, the nun insisted, and not likely to tell untruths. What Marcella was doing in a private avenue remains unexplained.

Another interesting suspect on Kennedy's list was 'Robert the painter'. He was from Belfast, but he knew his way around Whiteabbey having worked at a nearby mill. In 1949 Robert Taylor was an apprentice working for a painter called Barrett who got a job at the home of a Mrs. Minnie Magowan in Belfast. A Catholic, Mrs. Magowan was in her fifties and lived with her grown-up daughter Kathleen. Barrett found Taylor unreliable and sacked him.

Sometime later Taylor approached Mrs. Magowan and asked her to hire him to carry out some jobs. He said, untruthfully, that he had completed his decorator's apprenticeship. She said she would need to talk to Barrett first as he was her decorator. That came to nothing.

Meanwhile Taylor's girlfriend became pregnant, and he urgently needed money for a ring and a wedding. He set out for Mrs. Magowan's home on Ponsonby Avenue. When she answered the door, he asked to use her phone. She agreed and let him in. In the hall he tried to strangle her with a piece of strong cord, but she fought him off, and staggered into the scullery. He followed her and broke a bottle of holy water over her head. She fought back so he grabbed a carving knife and began to stab Mrs. Magowan and poured a pan of soup simmering on the stove all over her. To try to make sure that she was dead, he turned on the gas without lighting it and closed the scullery door.

In the kitchen he searched Mrs. Magowan's purse but found only small change. Through the window he could see his victim, despite her grievous injuries, stumbling around her back garden. A neighbour had seen her plight and was coming to her assistance over the garden wall. Taylor made himself scarce.

Against all expectations, Mrs. Magowan lived on for two days in hospital before her injuries overwhelmed her. She survived long enough for a young nurse to have the ghastly task of removing the partially cooked grains of barley from her open wounds, ingredients of the soup Taylor had thrown over her. Taylor had slipped out the front door unseen with less than one pound to show for his morning's dreadful work. Before she died of her injuries, Minnie Magowan identified the man who had attacked her. 'It was Robert the painter', she said.

But what had this to do with Patricia Curran's death? Lance Curran was then Northern Ireland's attorney general, and in court he led the prosecution against Robert Taylor. Taylor was a loyalist and despite compelling evidence against him, the jury split. A fellow loyalist and neighbour of Taylor's called MacConkey[iv] was a juryman and, against the evidence, refused to convict. The first jury was discharged because it could not deliver a unanimous verdict. A second trial was more successful, Taylor was convicted and sentenced to hang.

This time the prosecution thought that it had dealt with the problem of jury-tampering. The defence thought otherwise. It was the practice then to keep a jury locked up in police custody during such trials. To alleviate the monotony of a lengthy trial, the judge permitted the jury to go on supervised outings on days when there was no court sitting, provided they did not discuss the trial with anyone they might meet. A jury outing to Bangor to 'get fresh air' went as planned, but on a second one to Antrim town some jurymen had been permitted to mingle unsupervised with members of the public, and so, on appeal, the guilty verdict could not stand.

There could be no third trial.

Robert Taylor had got away with murder. He returned home to loyalist Tiger Bay in north Belfast to a hero's welcome. His release was hailed by loyalists who saw in it another well-deserved kick in the teeth for their nationalist neighbours. They celebrated with swaggering marching bands, anti-Catholic chanting, flags and bunting. The message was clear – no Belfast jury would hang a Protestant for murdering a Catholic.

Nationalists saw the outcome of the trial in the same stark terms and concluded that there was no rule of law in Northern Ireland, only mob rule. There was outrage that two trials in which the murderer had clearly been identified had led to his acquittal.

Two years later, the RUC, now investigating the murder of Patricia Curran, wondered if Taylor or his supporters could have targeted Lance Curran's daughter in retaliation for the attorney general's part in trying to convict Taylor. It was a legitimate line of inquiry, and Taylor's only alibi for the time of the murder was provided by members of his family. Added to which, the time of murder was not satisfactorily established, nor has it been since.

In a preliminary report to Sir Richard Pim in the days immediately following the murder, Inspector Kennedy also mentioned a very delicate matter. There was a significant discrepancy between what Judge Lance Curran said had happened on the night of the murder and that of other witnesses. The judge had phoned the home of John Steele, the student whom Patricia had met for a coffee on the afternoon before getting the bus home to Whiteabbey. Lance Curran said he had phoned between John Steele between 1.10am and 1.35am to ask if he knew where Patricia had gone the previous day. The judge then phoned the Davisons asking them to come over, mentioning that Steele had seen Patricia getting the 5pm bus to Whiteabbey. However, John Steele said that Lance Curran had phoned him at 2.10am. Steele's family confirmed that timing. The nub of that problem was conveyed in Kennedy's subsequent written report to Pim: 'If the call to the Steeles was not made until after 2pm, how could the Curran family have known that John Steele had left Patricia at the bus station at 5pm, unless Patricia herself had told them this?' This, of course, raised a very serious question. 'Had Patricia actually returned home and been murdered later in the evening and were the Currans fabricating a story?'[v] That discrepancy became apparent as early as 18 November 1952, according to Kennedy. It subsequently emerged that the RUC did not examine Patricia's bedroom until three days after her body had been found.

In any event, Sir Richard Pim had decided to send for the cavalry in the form of Scotland Yard. Pim was a loyal and committed servant of the British empire, and he had friends in high places upon whom he could call. The inspector general of the RUC, he was born in County Antrim in 1900, the son of a prominent Quaker who managed a linen firm. In

1918 Richard joined the Royal Naval Volunteer Reserve as a midshipman. After the war he read law at Trinity College, Dublin, and later joined the Royal Irish Constabulary. His service must have been short because that force ceased to exist in 1922.

A spell in the Northern Ireland civil service followed. Pim's big break came when Winston Churchill put him in charge of the map room at 10 Downing Street, the command centre of British forces between 1940 and 1945. Pim and his map room team accompanied Churchill on overseas travels, including numerous voyages and flights. During the enforced evacuation from Dunkirk in 1940, Pim volunteered to help because he thought his experience of small boats would be useful. Churchill was delighted with his subordinate's zeal. In early 1945, the map room team went to Yalta to support Churchill in talks with Franklin D. Roosevelt and Joseph Stalin, when the post-war settlement in Europe and other geo-political spheres of influence was negotiated. All this time spent together meant that Pim and Churchill became close, and a knighthood as Churchill left office in 1945 was one reward. Another was the post of inspector general of the Royal Ulster Constabulary. And when Pim needed doors opened in London in 1952, his friend Churchill, once again prime minister, was happy to oblige.

Pim had decided that Albert Kennedy and his RUC colleagues needed help in sorting out this most delicate investigation, and he approached the commissioner of the Metropolitan Police Sir Harold Scott for help. Scott agreed to lend him two good men with greater experience of handling murder inquiries than the Royal Ulster Constabulary.

It was probably the worst decision Richard Pim ever made in a lifetime of public service. Both his reputation and that of his senior detective – and successor – Albert Kennedy were damaged by it. It made good sense for a small police force to seek help from a larger one when faced with a case outside its normal range of experience, but here the involvement of London's Metropolitan Police turned a hitherto competent investigation into a travesty of justice which ruined the life of a vulnerable young man.

It is thought impolite to look gift horses in the mouth, but the newspapers devoting acres of paper and gallons of ink to their day-by-day coverage of this case should have looked a bit more closely at the senior Scotland Yard detective assigned to help the RUC. John Capstick had the reputation of being a copper's copper. That meant getting a result, no matter what corners had to be cut to achieve it. The criminal classes in London nicknamed Capstick Charley Artful and he took this as a compliment.

And the way in which Capstick's superiors in Scotland Yard deployed this hard-nosed detective was interesting, if anyone had cared to look. As he and his sergeant, Denis Hawkins, were getting ready to fly to Belfast, an unnamed colleague at Scotland Yard was briefing the London correspondents of the Belfast papers to the effect that although Capstick was London's best-known murder investigator, in Northern Ireland his job was to assist the RUC in tracking down the murderer, not to take over the investigation. Yet take it over he did, with disastrous results.

Capstick's main job was running Scotland Yard's 'Ghost Squad'. The name conjures up images of lantern-jawed detectives racing around London in high-powered cars with blue lights flashing and confronting determined bank robbers and safe-blowers, of burly men in crumpled suits standing on the steps of the Old Bailey when yet another 'old lag' had been sent down for ten years, and saying 'All in a day's work, guv' to gullible reporters.

The reality of the Ghost Squad was less impressive. When an investigation became bogged down, and a bit of 'muscle' was required, the Ghost Squad was summoned.

Capstick's experience in London, where wartime rationing, black market operations and criminals with weapons went hand-in-hand, made him a good reader of underworld operations. He enjoyed the cut-and-thrust of fighting crime in a big city. By Capstick's own admission, search warrants were a waste of time when a boot in the door or a helpful landlady was on hand, and people often became uncommonly helpful when John Capstick came on the scene. Those who were hitherto silent began to talk. Having got a confession by fair means or foul, the Ghost Squad then withdrew. Regular detectives concluded the investigation and presented the evidence. A corollary of this is that Capstick did not often have to appear in court where his rough-and-ready approach might be a weakness. The danger existed that a clever defence lawyer could elicit damaging admissions. In Capstick's ghost-written memoir he defended his approach to the Curran murder investigation: 'I took the only course open to me'. The title of the memoir *Given in Evidence* now appears to be a bad joke.

Coincidentally, John Capstick and his wife Barbara had been on a short holiday in Ireland when Patricia Curran was murdered. The Dublin newspapers made hay with the story, and Capstick said he read every word. Holiday over, on the Monday he went back to work in Scotland Yard, and was instructed to report immediately to Sir Ronald Howe, assistant commissioner for crime. Howe came to the point immediately.

'Sir Richard Pim has asked for our assistance on the Curran murder. I think you're the right man for the job. Take Detective-Sergeant Hawkins with you and get the first available plane for Belfast. Don't leave a pebble unturned. This is as ghastly a murder as any I've ever known. Stay in Ireland until the murderer has been brought to justice.'[vi]

The assistant commissioner's stricture about leaving no pebble unturned was probably not required. In 1948, investigating the murder of toddler June Anne Devaney in Lancashire, Capstick had the entire male population of the town of Blackburn, more than 4, 000 men and boys over sixteen, fingerprinted. Unconventional yes, illegal probably but nevertheless effective. A man named Peter Griffiths was hanged for the murder in Walton Prison in Liverpool on 19 November 1948.

Originally from Aintree, near Liverpool, Capstick ran away to sea at the age of sixteen. A phrenologist examined the young man's head and told his proud mother: 'Madam your son will either be a great detective or a great thief.' Capstick later said that prompted him and a friend to travel down to London to join the Metropolitan Police, which paid better than the Liverpool constabulary.

On his first days in uniform in a seedy part of London, a senior colleague told Capstick to always keep his thumb in the strap of his truncheon, ready for action. 'Johnny Wood is the copper's best friend', he was told. Capstick had served more than twenty years as a policeman in 1952, and he was just about to turn fifty years of age.

'Scotland Yard experts reconstruct crime' the *Belfast Newsletter* told readers on 18 November, over a photograph of three weary-looking middle-aged men in suits at Belfast airport, then a former RAF base called Nutt's Corner. The photograph showed Capstick, Hawkins and Kennedy outside the airport building on the previous night. Inspector Kennedy briefed his guests, 'going into all aspects of the murder of Miss Patricia Curran in the grounds of her father's house', readers were told. Together the trio had then visited the place where her body was found. 'Today they will assist in further investigations and, it is hoped, they will be able to throw some new light on the crime and suggest steps which will ultimately lead to the apprehension of the murderer', the inspector general of the RUC told reporters.

Pim explained he had sought outside help because of the enormous public anxiety about the murder. 'In spite of several days of widespread investigation the police were unable to make an arrest in that tragic case although members of the force had given long hours of unremitting service in following up many lines of inquiry.' Albert Kennedy would remain in charge of the investigation with the assistance of the two Scotland Yard detectives, Pim insisted. So far, no weapon had been recovered and no motive for the murder had been found. Nor had a man who had been seen in a café in Carrickfergus with traces of hay sticking out of his hair responded to a police appeal to come forward.

Pim asked for information about a black Austin car, seen driving from Whiteabbey towards Belfast by a taximan, Frank Stephenson, who had dropped the judge home at about 7.15pm on the night his daughter went missing. Curious about the car and its high speed, Stephenson had followed it. 'All the way to Belfast he [the driver] appeared to be in a hurry and anxious that I should not catch up. At the junction of North Queen Street and York Road I lost contact.'

The following morning, newspapers reported on a press conference in Whiteabbey attended by Kennedy and the two Scotland Yard detectives. The scope of the inquiries had been widened, Kennedy told the press. Descriptions of people the police wanted to talk to had been circulated in the Irish Republic as well as Northern Ireland, he said, and the possibility that the crime could have been committed by a woman had not been ruled out. (This was probably a Capstick intervention. Privately he was of the opinion that the weapon, described as stiletto-like by the pathologist, was more likely to have been used by a female or a foreigner. Real men used more manly weapons, in Capstick's opinion.)

'Mr. Justice Curran and Mrs. Curran, whose daughter Patricia was murdered in the grounds of Glen House, Whiteabbey, on 12 November, have left their home for a short rest', the *Belfast Newsletter* told readers on the morning of 20 November. Some accounts said they went to Scotland for a few days. In any event, the Currans never returned to live in Glen House.

Figure 2: Patricia Curran in the centre with her father Lance on the left. Her brother Michael is partially obscured top left, and Desmond is behind her smiling broadly seen on the right.

Meanwhile members of the public had been handing in knives and daggers to RUC stations. The police had spoken to friends of Patricia Curran, some of whom had worked with her in the engineering company, but none was a suspect, according to Kennedy.

By then the police checked out the Whiteabbey schoolgirl Marcella Devlin's statement about the scar-faced man and had decided to take it seriously, without citing her as the source. The *Belfast Newsletter* speculated that because the police statement mentioned two coats, there was more than one witness, and nobody said otherwise.

The next day's headlines were a bit more exciting. 'Search for scar-faced man', the *Belfast Newsletter* proclaimed. 'In connection with the murder of Patricia Curran, it is desired to interview a man aged about 30 years, about 6ft tall, with a noticeable old scar on the left side of his face between eye and mouth. This man has been seen wearing a soft hat of American style with a wide brim and may be wearing a fawn raincoat or grey herring-bone overcoat' a police statement said, published on 21 November.

Other leads were drying up. The driver of the speeding black Austin car had not come forward. And Mrs Gorman, the Carrickfergus café owner who reported the suspicious-looking customer with hay in his hair had received a letter from Nottingham. The writer said he was that customer and assured her that he had nothing to do with the murder. The police in Nottingham were checking, and he dropped out of the picture.

Saturday's papers had little to add, apart from speculation that the investigation was focused on the search for an unspecified missing article that Miss Curran had acquired soon after she became a university student. This, it later transpired, was a fencing foil she had bought, and it was rumoured that it could have been the murder weapon, but the police ruled this out.

By Monday, 24 November, a second weekend had passed since the murder, and if the daily press conferences were any indicator, little progress had been made. A police statement issued the previous day reiterated the call for information on the scar-faced man and added to it a request for a cyclist to come forward. He had stopped in Whiteabbey around 5.25pm on Wednesday, 12 November to attend to a flat tyre. The police also said that Patricia Curran's diaries had been examined but had yielded nothing useful to their investigation. Some thirty women in Whiteabbey had got together to provide one another with escorts when attending events which took place after dark.

Back at the RAF base in Edenmore, where the police had established a temporary barracks in a girls' training centre, the investigations continued. Iain Hay Gordon was interviewed by RAF police on Thursday and Friday (13 and 14 November) and his letters home give us part of the picture. He was in the habit of writing at least twice a week, once to each parent. His father Douglas, a mining engineer, worked much of the time away from home.

Iain Gordon's letters that survive are formal and often repetitive, but they show a greater command of language, spelling and grammar than one might expect of a youth whose education had so often been interrupted. Here in a letter to his father who was working in south Wales, dated Sunday, 16 November, three days after Patricia Curran's body was found, he writes about the murder and his connection with the Curran family and how that made him feel:

> You may have heard on the wireless or read in the newspapers that Patricia Curran, the 19-year-old daughter of Mr Justice Curran, a NI high court judge, was brutally murdered. I knew the girl slightly and the family, especially her brother Desmond, so I do not feel too good. She was found in the grounds of their house, stabbed to

death. Patricia had 22 wounds in her. Her father had been a Northern Ireland high court judge for two years and at the funeral was a grief-stricken man. At the inquest, I believe it was stated that she was raped, strangled and stabbed, but please do not say that to anyone as it is unofficial.[vii]

Patricia was one of the nicest girls that I have had the good fortune to know. She was so nice and polite, quiet and helpful that she was a perfect joy to know. Patricia Curran was the last person that you would have thought anyone would wish to harm. I knew her only slightly; you are not in the best of spirits when an acquaintance of yours is killed.

There is nothing that I – and many, many others – would not do to see that nice young girl restored to life again. But that can never be, we just have a memory but what a sweet fragrant memory it is. I want to see the worker of this iniquitous deed brought to justice, not for vengeance's sake but so that the murderer may be made to pay for his dastardly foul crime. I was deeply upset and profoundly shocked by it all.

Gordon also told his father that some time ago Desmond Curran had invited him to visit the Curran home, and he had gone there three times. It is significant that in this letter he does not mention that the RAF military police had already questioned him twice about his movements on the night of the murder.

On the following Wednesday, Iain Gordon wrote to his father again. He complained that his father had not replied to the previous letter. There is a greater urgency to this letter. He was clearly rattled and needed to get something off his chest.

… there is not much to tell you except for one very important thing. You remember what I said to you in my previous letter about the murder in Whiteabbey? Since then I have been interviewed by the RAF police and by the RUC. Everybody was interviewed by the RAF police. On Monday the RUC questioned me no less than three times. They were up at camp at mid-day and in the afternoon, I was at Whiteabbey police barracks, and there a statement was taken from me regarding my movements on Wednesday and my relationship with the Curran family. As if that was not enough, they were up at Edenmore in the evening. This is all because I was acquainted with the family of the deceased girl and they are, I fancy, hoping that I will be able to give them a lead, but I was useless to them as I knew the girl so slightly. The police are checking on every word and phrase in my statement and are extremely anxious that I verify that I was in the billet between five and six pm, or in the billet after tea until I went to the registry. I was not out at all except when I posted the mail between 4 and 4.30pm. Nobody can verify that I was in the billet then, and unfortunately it was at that time, it is believed, that the murder was committed. I was not questioned yesterday but I believe that one of the NAAFI [military canteen] girls was asked what time I came into the NAAFI She was asked the same question on Monday. As far as I am concerned there is nothing at all to worry about, but I shall be relieved when the murderer is arrested and charged with the murder of Patricia Curran. I, of course, anything of a serious nature arises, I will notify you at once.

We know that Gordon was interviewed by the RAF police on Thursday 13 November and the next day, and probably by the RUC on the Saturday as well, but after that dates become confused. Gordon may be wrong in telling his father that police interviewed him three times on Monday,17 November. That was probably the following day when Capstick's colleague Hawkins was spending his first day at Edenmore.

Brenda Gordon became alarmed at this turn of events. She was unable to get away, so she asked her husband to go over to Belfast and see how Iain was. Douglas Gordon had also noticed the tone of agitation in his elder son's letters and got on a ferry. He arrived early on Saturday morning 22 November. He saw Iain first, then Hawkins. He told the detective sergeant that his son was a nervous type, inclined to worry, and he showed him Iain's letters about the murder investigation. Hawkins took the letters, read them and handed them back. He laughed and assured Douglas Gordon that neither he nor his son had anything to worry about. Douglas Gordon phoned his wife to put her mind at ease then returned to Cheshire where he was working at the time.

When first questioned about his whereabouts in the aftermath of the murder, Iain Hay Gordon had a very noticeable black eye which he claimed was the result of 'scrapping' in the barracks. Leaving aside the murder investigation, Gordon was – at the very least – accident-prone and subject to bullying by his fellow airmen.

In many ways he was immature for a 20-year-old. He certainly didn't get on well with his fellow conscripts, who thought him an oddball. In the messroom and the billet, he tended to avoid contact with other conscripts.

Making young men serve in the armed forces after leaving school continued in the UK until 1960. With two world wars in recent memory, it was thought necessary for national defence, and there was a general view that being in the military for a spell either knocked the stuffing out of a young fellow, or made a man out of him, depending on your point of view.

All that is certain is that eighteen months in the Royal Air Force did this young Scot few favours. An unprepossessing, skinny young man, he avoided the company of his fellow conscripts by getting up and dressing himself earlier than they did. He spent many evenings alone writing letters to his parents. For example, on the night that Patricia Curran was murdered, almost all the soldiers had gone to an armed forces' dance in Belfast. All except Gordon. It was a pity that the RAF did not take a little more interest in this misfit conscript, because he had the makings of a good medium-distance runner and had been a member of a running club back home in Dollar, Clackmannanshire, where his parents had sent him to a 'good' school, though his academic record there was patchy.

Had some NCO or officer been more observant, Gordon's time at Edenmore might have been more agreeable and his development less stunted.

Prompted by his mother's letters encouraging him to meet people outside the camp, he had been going once a week to Betty Staff's, a popular dance salon in Ann Street, Belfast, where he learned some steps., He then met a nurse, Gay Brooke from the Royal Victoria Hospital at a nightclub in Belfast, and thereafter they often went to the cinema together until he went home on leave at the end of 1952.

That left the one strong interest in Gordon' life – religion. In his teenage years this interest had blossomed, his mother later said. At home in Scotland he had been a lay reader at church services. In Northern Ireland he went twice on Sundays to the large Presbyterian church which dominated the coastline at Whiteabbey, where the Curran family also worshipped.

In camp most of Gordon's free time was spent in the office or central registry, as it was known. When he went back there after working hours, he said he was practising typing for an upcoming examination, though his letters which survive are hand-written.

Two years of National Service was supposed to equip conscripts with a trade or skill with which to make their way in the world when they left. As 1952 drew to a close, Gordon had six months left to serve, being due out in May 1953, and had to sit what were described as 'trade examinations' before he finished

It is possible to read into Gordon's letters to his father an element of 'marking his card, of preparing him for what might come. The young man knew that he was vulnerable. It was only a matter of time before the police got wind of his sexual dabbling. Gordon had visited prostitutes in Belfast and had homosexual relations with a barber in Newtownabbey. Even a suggestion of homosexuality was risky, and Gordon would not have wanted his parents to hear about it. The fear of being exposed and the risk of being blackmailed was an ever-present reality. Today for young men to have feelings for one another is unremarkable, but up to 1967 homosexuality was a criminal offence in Britain and a spell in prison as a sex offender was much to be feared. Homosexuals had been executed as recently as 1835, when two men were hanged outside London's Newgate prison for 'the abominable crime of buggery'.

In Northern Ireland male homosexuality remained illegal until 1982, after the European Court of Human Rights struck down the criminalisation of homosexual acts between consenting adults, following a lawsuit by campaigner Jeff Dudgeon.

Until Patricia Curran's murderer had been apprehended, Gordon knew he had to keep Desmond Curran on his side. Desmond had his own secrets. As will become clear in what follows, the two young men had been friends for nearly a year, discussing matters of faith and conscience, including

Gordon's homosexual encounters with Wesley Courtney, the Newtownabbey barber, and Curran had told his RUC friend Deveney about this. Then a detective sergeant in the RUC, Samuel Deveney had been on duty collecting evidence at the place where Patricia's body was found. He continued to be closely involved in the subsequent investigation, was present during the autopsy and later played a part in an interrogation of Gordon which helped to secure a confession. After Gordon had confessed but before he had signed it, Deveney broke police regulations by speaking to him and he also collated exhibits for Gordon's trial. Ubiquitous does not begin to describe Deveney's part in the investigation of Patricia Curran's murder.

At this point Desmond Curran was also a possible suspect and Deveney was disclosing confidential police information to him. Rather than being sanctioned for this, Deveney was promoted from sergeant to head constable by the time he came to give evidence in March 1953.

Two days before Christmas 1952 and disregarding his parents' advice to stay well away from the Curran family, Iain Gordon phoned Desmond Curran. 'He asked if I could meet him that evening and I met him about 8pm … I took notes of the conversation immediately on my return home' Curran said. According to Gordon, he had phoned Curran to arrange to see him to return a pound (sterling), then a sizeable sum, which he had borrowed from him earlier to pay for shoe repairs.

That conversation, which began at eight o'clock at the Val d'Or café in Wellington Place, Belfast, would be a lengthy one. Desmond Curran described what happened in a written statement he gave to Samuel Deveney: 'We met in the café and Gordon sympathised with me, and we had some general conversation. Then he asked me if I would like to go somewhere else where we could talk. I suggested the Presbyterian Hostel in Howard Street. He said there was a small lounge which would be suitable. We got into a lift to go [up] to the lounge. We were alone in the lift and he said: "Now we go up to the heavens". Then he turned pale, and it seemed to me that he said: "Someone will be asleep in five minutes".' (Gordon later told doctors that he was subject to occasional 'blackouts', and this was one of them.)

Curran asked Gordon what he thought of the murder. Gordon replied that he did not really know Patricia well enough to say. 'The [Presbyterian Hostel] lounge was occupied, and I suggested that we walk and talk at the same time. Gordon said we could go in the Malone Road direction, and he seemed anxious we should go to our new home [in south Belfast].'

Gordon then described his difficulties about the police questioning his alibi, and of being at the camp at 5pm on the day of the murder. He also complained that police in Scotland had been questioning his mother.

In the account Desmond Curran wrote afterwards of his meeting with Gordon in Belfast on 23 December 1952, there is clearly a secret between the two men which is not being stated. One had a hold over the other, but we cannot tell who had the upper hand. In fact, they had a mutual interest in keeping something under wraps, homosexuality on which they were both vulnerable. Curran had disclosed Gordon's encounters with Courtney to his RUC friend, against Gordon's wishes. However, Curran chose not to reveal that in the written account of their meeting:

He apologised [to me] for not having written …
he said later that his parents had told him not to
contact the Curran family. He asked what I had
told the police about him. I said I had told them
everything I knew. He said he had done the same
about me, even some things he didn't want to tell.
He asked me if I had told the police every single

thing that would help. I said yes. He said that he sworn he had. He emphasised the word sworn.

Gordon asked Curran if he would answer some questions and Curran said yes. Gordon then asked if her family usually knew where Patricia was and who she was with:

I said that we did but not the exact time of her comings and goings. He said that it was strange that on that particular day we did not know where she was or who she was with. He suggested that it was strange and risky for her to work for a firm of contractors. Why had she done so, and what had been the reactions of my mother and father? I said that I did not think it was strange or risky, and she had done so partly for experience and partly for pocket money. I said that my mother had not liked it, but my father had not objected. He asked me if she [Patricia] was in the habit of visiting low parts of the town out of curiosity and I said no.

In this part of their conversation, Gordon suggested that the motive for murdering Patricia had been fear. She was murdered because 'she had found out something about someone', Gordon said. Fear of disclosure was clearly in the air.

The two men ate supper at the Presbyterian Hostel, and Curran walked with Gordon to the bus station where he took the 11pm bus to Edenmore. It must have been a companionable evening for them. They met in a café, visited a hostel, walked around much of south Belfast, ate supper together, spending fully three hours in each other's company.

Curran went home to write an account of the evening while it was still fresh in his mind. Gordon later challenged the accuracy of that written statement. The evening together was over, but their discussion was not. At the end of it, the two men arranged to meet again six days later, on Monday 29 December. In the event Gordon phoned Curran to say that he could not get away from Edenmore on that day. He phoned again later on Monday to say that he could meet Curran after all. But by then Curran was not free. In the interim he had arranged to see Samuel Deveney. Curran told Gordon that he was passing on certain information [about homosexuality] to the policeman. This upset Gordon because he tried to phone Curran the following day, Tuesday 30 December, to find out what was said between him and his policemen friend. He didn't get through but Curran phoned Gordon back later the same day to tell him that he had no reason to worry.

We now switch to Gordon's account of what passed between the two men. His first – and the most significant of three letters to Curran in a six-day period – was dated Tuesday 30 December 1952, the day he tried to find out what had Curran said to Deveney about their homosexual behaviour. In its handwritten form, the letter ran to 11 pages. He was about to go home to Scotland for Hogmanay, but he sent this letter from Edenmore:

Tuesday 30 December 1952

Dear Desmond

I have just come off the phone with you and hope that your discussion [with detective Samuel Deveney] went all right last night. I am only too glad to have been of help and if anything occurs in the future, I will, of course, let you know. I will spare no effort on my part to help you, but once again, Desmond, I must stress that I know nothing that can be of any real importance. What I told you is the last piece of information that I had, and quite frankly I do not think it is or was of any real importance. I think what you have told me bears me out on that point. But if I do think of anything or find anything out, I will inform you straight away. You have my word on that score.

Before I write any more, I wish to tell you before I forget, will you please give my best regards to your family. I will write to you every day that I am away and when I'm in Ireland I will write and/or phone every day. But I will not take this course of action until I hear from you.

I would be very grateful if you destroyed all my correspondence on this score as it could be of real importance. Another thing I don't want you to mention to anyone is my address in Scotland.

I was glad that you said that I would not be involved for I am thinking primarily of my position in the RAF, and more important still, of my parents. I do not wish to cause them any more worry and being in the RAF, you will realise, puts me in a tight spot.

As far as telling that information to the policeman [Deveney] is concerned, I maybe should have insisted you informed me first or I should be annoyed, but under the circumstances I can say nothing. You must be guided solely, Desmond, by what you think best and right, no matter what is involved. But, in future, could you inform me first? But that is not likely to happen as I know nothing more, but if I do think of anything else, I will, as I have said, let you know. Do you think, Desmond, that if you have any more conversation with your friend you will speak as highly of me as possible, and give me as good and as high a character as is possible? Of course, speak the truth at all times. That advice though will be unnecessary to you. I hope that everything is going all right and that your Moral Re-Armament is going according to plan.

As you told me about your dreams, I will tell you about one I had on Sunday night or in the early hours of Monday morning [Sunday night 28 December-Monday morning 29 December]. As you know the nights are very clear and light due to the clear moon and absence of cloud. As soon as I had it, I tried to relate it [commit it?] to memory but in the morning, I am afraid I was rather hazy, as is the way with dreams. I have great difficulty in remembering the bare details.

I was sleeping in a large house in a bedroom, and somebody woke me up and said that something terrible had happened as there was a woman screaming … and we ran into a woman's bedroom and found a woman, fairly young in years, in a horrible state, strangled. I said we had better get help and as I ran out, I woke up.

I tried to think to what it could refer and at once thought of Patricia but did not see any obvious connection. I looked out of the window at the head of my bed, and everything was lovely and clear in the moonlight. There was not a soul about and at the other end of the billet someone's curtains seemed to blow back for no obvious reason unless his window was open. I tried to keep awake and thought hard but fell off to sleep – I must have fallen to sleep straight away.

In the morning, when I tried to think about it, my mind was hazy. Could the reason for the dream be that I have been thinking about this affair a lot for some other reason that I do not know? But as this is only my second dream since May 1951, when I was conscripted into the RAF, I am just wondering. That is about all I can say. I think of it all the time, always racking my brain to see if there is not something that has not occurred to me, and always nothing fresh occurs to me. But I am confident that in God's good time, justice will be done. It will not be an unsolved case – of that I am confident.

Now if you will excuse me, I must close, and I apologise for the bad writing and bad English, but I wrote this in one awful hurry, and did it as I am, as you know, only too anxious to help. If my mother and father knew what I was doing, I am sure they would shoot me, but that is between you and me. I will spare no effort to help.

But I must close. I hope I have not taken up too much of your valuable time. I will be thinking of you and will remember you in my prayers. So, in the meantime, all the best and I will be delighted to hear from you.

Your sincerely
Iain Hay Gordon

Gordon wrote a short reminder letter to Curran the following day from his aunt's house in Rutherglen, Glasgow, trying to prompt a reply. He concluded by wishing the Curran family a happy new year. 'I hope you have received my letter and will act upon my instructions. Will you please keep me informed and will you please destroy this letter when you have read it as it can be of no value?'

Curran's reply must have arrived in the meantime because on 4 January 1953, Gordon wrote: 'It was good of you to write, and I was considerably heartened and relieved to have it. I will be returning shortly to NI and will write or telephone then.'

That concluded the exchange of letters, so far as the available records show, but Gordon had promised to remain in daily contact with Curran either by phone or by letter.

What are we to make of Gordon's side of the new year exchange with Curran, beginning with the time they spent together before Christmas and continuing through phone calls and increasingly agitated letters into early January? There are two clear strands. First Gordon's concern about what Curran disclosed to Deveney – which we now know to be the secret the two men shared over homosexuality – and perhaps some knowledge they had about Patricia's death which they could not disclose either without incriminating themselves? But the second point – the dream sequence in which a young woman is murdered – is significant. Dreams are just dreaming for most people, but why did Gordon spell out a dream in which he may be asleep in a bedroom in a big house similar to Glen House, while a young woman is being murdered? Is he reminding Desmond Curran of something that happened in a bed at his parents' house? Gordon's visits to the Curran home were not all at lunchtime. The bedrooms were accessible at ground level at the back of the house due to the sloping site, and one could enter or leave Patricia's bedroom through the window.

There is a clear threat in Gordon's recounting of the dream. Though the wording is almost poetic– the fluttering curtain – he is reminding that they share a secret, perhaps more than one, better not revealed. And if Curran can speak out of turn to a member of the police, so also can Gordon.

And Gordon in all of this addressed Curran in a very familiar way, the way close friends often do. At one stage he bids Curran to follow his instructions. How could Desmond Curran, Cambridge scholar and Queen's University law graduate, on the threshold of what was expected to be a brilliant career in the law and perhaps become a judge like his father – take instructions from Iain Hay Gordon, a low-ranking RAF conscript, in class-conscious Northern Ireland in the 1950s, unless there was a strong bond between the two men?

Some commentators see in this exchange support for their theory that though Gordon did not murder Patricia Curran, he might have been an accessory helping to conceal evidence, and thus felt vulnerable. Had Desmond asked Gordon to dispose of some piece of evidence perhaps? And that the police, knowing or suspecting this, took a sceptical view of Gordon's testimony, suspecting that he must be involved in some way. One policeman, in particular, learning of these exchanges, smelt a rat, or thought he had.

Much of this did not emerge until Gordon was examined in Holywell Asylum in 1957 by an independent doctor, nominated by the British Home Office, when the campaign for his release was gaining momentum. 'As regards his sex life, Gordon said he had his first sexual experience in the summer of 1952 with two prostitutes, and in the latter half of 1952 he had been the passive partner in a case of buggery with C [Courtney] on two or three occasions and with D [Desmond] on one', the external doctor's report said. By coincidence that doctor examining Gordon was also called Desmond Curran. Dr. Curran concluded those incidents were 'adolescent transient phenomena' and did not mean that Gordon was primarily homosexual.

Brenda Gordon thought her son was listless and slept a lot during his visit home for Hogmanay. On the day before he was due to return to Ireland, he had opened up a bit to her. He had been thinking about what he might do when he was discharged from the RAF, he said. He now felt he might like to stay in Northern Ireland. Though barracks life was disagreeable, it would soon be over, and he thought he might move back into the Presbyterian Hostel in south Belfast. He spent a week there before being sent to Edenmore, and he liked it and had made friends there. He would sign up for a commercial college course and get a job as a clerk. 'I could not imagine Iain in an office, but I was so glad that he had made up his mind at last that I threw myself into the discussion and we sat and talked of his future', she wrote later.

For much of what had remained of 1952, the murder investigation had attracted little press coverage. Brief updates barely added to what was already known. On Saturday 29 November the *Belfast Newsletter* said that Lance Curran had written letters of thanks to all who had responded to his family's appeal for information, and he wanted to say that he was grateful to the anonymous informants too.

There had been a flurry of press interest at the beginning of December when a man in Manchester confessed to the murder of Patricia Curran. Kennedy and Capstick flew over to question him and concluded that the informant was an attention-seeker and that they had been victims of a hoax. Throughout December police inquiries continued. Gordon was questioned again twice but stuck to his false alibi.

On 17 December 1952 Capstick travelled to Dublin to discuss the investigation with the Garda Síochána to see if there was any connection between the Curran murder and a case they were investigating. There was none and so he returned to Belfast where he and Hawkins prepared to go home for Christmas.

A couple of days before Christmas, the RUC finally got around to taking a statement from Patricia's mother with an unnamed lawyer present, but what Doris Curran said to them remains in a closed file. It would be interesting to know why a grieving mother was not questioned until more than a month after the murder, in the presence of a lawyer, and on the eve of her first Christmas without her daughter.

On the last day of 1952, Sir Richard Pim announced a reward of £1,000 for information leading to the arrest of the murderer. That was a substantial sum, more than £25,000 in current values.

Figure 3: Whiteabbey, the Shore Road, the telephone box is where Patricia Curran usually phoned home for a lift up the avenue.

As 1953 began, two apparent leads emerged. 'Scar-faced man attacked 22-year-old Miss Roberta Bradley' the *Northern Whig* reported on 5 January. Inspector Albert Kennedy was quoted as saying that the RUC was looking into possible connections between this attack and the Curran murder. That lead dried up as quickly as it had appeared, but it prompted the police to appeal again for information about a man emerging from the avenue on to Shore Road on the day of the murder.

'RUC ask Dutch police to search for 21-year-old seaman in connection with Curran murder' the *Northern Whig* told its readers three days later. A seaman called Bartold Schuitema from the Netherlands had 'jumped ship' in Dublin and made his way north where he came under suspicion. This sounded like a promising lead, but he was quickly eliminated from police inquiries. John Capstick told some of his Fleet Street contacts that he was not going to stay much longer in Belfast. That at least was true, though perhaps not in the way that most people expected.

When Iain Gordon returned to Belfast, he did so via Dublin, and travelling north first-class on the Enterprise express train. It was Saturday night, and he stayed in the Presbyterian Hostel, but first he attended a dance at Belfast Technical College where he met a girl called Elma Ewart who was a neighbour of Albert Kennedy. He returned to Edenmore the following day, attended evening service at Whiteabbey, and had tea afterwards with Reverend McCappin, the Church of Ireland rector of Whiteabbey, who had invited him and some other young people. On Monday he began work again, and, in the evening, he met a young woman he knew called Betty Hagan, and they attended a play 'Johnny Comes Marching Home' staged by an amateur drama group. On Tuesday morning he was ordered to report to Sergeant Hawkins, and on Wednesday the morning post brought him two 'Dear John' letters. Both Betty Hagan and

Gaye Brooke said much the same thing, very politely – 'It has been nice knowing you Iain, but that's over now; please don't contact me again'.

Capstick and Hawkins had returned to Belfast in January 1953 knowing that time was passing, and they had no progress to report. Iain Gordon was back in the barracks at Edenmore, and Desmond Curran was practising law and living in south Belfast with his father, mother and brother Michael.

Capstick and Hawkins were due to leave Northern Ireland soon, and something had to happen – quickly. Deveney briefed Capstick about the exchanges between Desmond Curran and Iain Gordon around Christmas and the Scotland Yard detective's interest was piqued. 'I decided the time had come to act', Capstick said. 'If this outwardly normal boy were indeed a murderer, he was no ordinary criminal. But it could be that he was living some curious, secret life of which he showed no trace to the world. It could be that his passion for study, his desperate anxiety to make a success of his career had unbalanced him and made him a danger to the world.'

So Capstick instructed Detective Sergeant Hawkins and Head Constable Samuel Russell of the RUC to interrogate Gordon at length. 'I want to know everything about him', he told the officers. 'His childhood, his private habits, his attitude towards girls, his friendship with the Curran family, and above all the whole truth about his movements on the evening of the murder.'

The RAF camp commandant Richard Popple was informed that Gordon should present himself for questioning. Popple responded by telling Hawkins that an RAF officer must be present if an underage man (Gordon was twenty, and so not legally an adult) was being asked to give a written statement about a criminal offence. Hawkins chose to ignore this.

Thus began what was either three days of routine inquiries and voluntary statements made by Iain Hay Gordon in the normal course of a murder inquiry, with adequate breaks for meals, or a barrage of continuous interrogations involving relays of twelve or thirteen policemen intended to break down a vulnerable man and force him into making damaging admissions, depending on who you believe, Capstick or Gordon.

On Tuesday 13 January 1953, in the opening session at the temporary police barracks at Edenmore, Hawkins questioned Gordon for 90 minutes with no one else present, telling him that he wanted to ask him about his own family, his background, his habits and his relationship with the Curran family. The first hour consisted of what Hawkins described as a general conversation, and then he began taking down a statement from Gordon, in answer to questions he put to him. At around 11.30.am, they were joined by RUC Head Constable Samuel Russell, who assisted in the interview until they broke for lunch at 12.15 p.m. According to the defence, Russell followed Gordon on his way to the barracks for lunch in order to continue to harass and put pressure on him. Russell denied this, though he admitted speaking to Gordon on his way to lunch.

After lunch, Gordon returned at 2.30pm (the prosecution said it was 3pm) when the interrogation continued, going over familiar ground: how Gordon came to know Desmond and the Curran family, how Gordon had met a nurse from the Royal Victoria Hospital in Belfast, and they had gone out together on certain Monday nights. 'I am still friendly with her. I would not describe her as my girlfriend', Gordon had said. 'We have not fallen out.' According to Hawkins, the murder was not discussed on that first day, but the latter part of that first day's statement indicates that homosexuality *was* raised and there was a long discussion about Gordon's sex life. Gordon spoke of being approached by a homosexual. 'I have no inclination that way, and as far as I know, neither has Desmond. I still continue to be friendly with Desmond', he told the two policemen. Statement-taking continued until four o'clock in the afternoon, according to the police. The defence said it was five o'clock. Gordon signed the statement and left. The statement was 800 words long at this stage.

The defence maintained that other unidentified officers were brought into the interrogation to put pressure on Gordon, but Hawkins denied that. Officers might have entered the room to bring messages to colleagues present such as 'you are wanted on the phone' during questioning, but they took no part in the interrogation, he said. Gordon later indicated that he had no great problem with the way in which the police handled matters on that first day, except that the questioning lasted much longer than they said.

On Wednesday 14 January, Gordon returned to the temporary police barracks to complete his statement. Again, the Edenmore commander, while giving permission for Gordon to attend, raised the question of having an RAF officer present, and once more it was not acted upon. Hawkins later denied this under oath, but he cannot be regarded as a reliable witness on the matter.

There was another irregularity. Capstick intercepted Gordon on his way to the temporary police barracks in the morning and spoke to him for some time – ten minutes according to Capstick– with nobody else present before resumption of the previous day's questioning was resumed. Hawkins claimed to know nothing of this intervention by his superior officer and went so far as to say it had not taken place. The defence's contention that Gordon was being held for three days and subjected to a series of 'ambushes' by policemen other than those formally identified as questioning him was beginning to look credible.

After Capstick had finished with Gordon, Hawkins and Russell then jointly questioned him about his movements on the day of the murder. He admitted for the first time what most people had known since the beginning, that his alibi for the day of the murder between 5pm and 6pm had been concocted at the suggestion of the RAF internal police. This admission placed Gordon in trouble twice over – once because he now admitted that he had told a lie – and secondly because he now had no alibi for the hours between 5pm and 6pm on the day of the murder which the police maintained, with conditional support from the autopsy result, had taken place between 5.30pm and 6pm.

The morning interrogation continued until 1.30pm without a break, and by then the lunch service at Whiteabbey was over. Hawkins said he told Gordon that he could accompany him and Russell to Belfast for lunch. Gordon agreed and they went either to the Courts of Justice restaurant to eat, or the Crown Bar in Great Victoria Street, depending on whose account you believe. Gordon was in uniform, the two detectives in plain clothes.

During the meal, there was no let-up for Gordon, he said. The formal questioning resumed at three o'clock back at the barracks and at four o'clock Gordon's statement admitting that he lied about his alibi was completed. Gordon read it over then signed it at 4.30p.m., according to Hawkins. At this point Capstick reappeared and spoke to Gordon on his own for a further unstated period of time, perhaps two hours, before Gordon was allowed to go back to the barracks. That was around 7p.m. according to Gordon and it was partially confirmed by a fellow conscript called Brown who saw him returning to his billet. Gordon himself gave a harrowing account of being bullied and shouted at by Russell in particular. He was dismissed for the day much earlier according to the police, and the bullying and shouting complained of never took place.

At the end of the second day of interrogation, Gordon had been in close police custody from around 9.30am to 6pm or 7pm and under formal interrogation for all but an hour of that time. His alibi was in ribbons, his credibility likewise and he had shown acute vulnerability when questioned on the subject of homosexuality. He was now in serious trouble.

On the morning of the third day of interrogation, Thursday 15 January, when Gordon turned up at the temporary police barracks, Hawkins was waiting for him. He told Gordon that Capstick would be there soon to question him. During the 30 minutes before Capstick arrived, Gordon was alone with Hawkins; then District Inspector Nelson entered the room to allow Hawkins 'to take a telephone call'; he returned sometime later. Before the day was out, Gordon would be interrogated by the three policemen leading the investigation, Capstick, Kennedy and Hawkins, have at least three other exchanges with other policemen, at which no notes were made, and eventually confess to murder.

Capstick must have felt confident that his investigation was over because *The Irish Times* reported on the Thursday that the two Scotland Yard men were finishing up in Northern Ireland at the end of that week. To have been published in the newspaper on 15 January, that statement had to have been made before the three-day interrogation had been completed.

The following day newspapers reported the sensational arrest of Iain Hay Gordon, and that he had been charged with Patricia Curran's murder at a special court in Whiteabbey and remanded in custody by resident magistrate Dr. Mills. That a knife was found on the foreshore at Whiteabbey a couple of days later must have confirmed the public's perception that Scotland Yard, like the Mounties, had got their man.

When Gordon appeared on remand at Whiteabbey, a week later, some 300 women waited an hour outside the

Royal Legion hall, the temporary court premises, hoping to catch a glimpse of him. Capstick and Hawkins were back in Northern Ireland for the taking of depositions on Wednesday, 4 February 1953, when the main prosecution witness was Desmond Curran, who gave his account of his pre-Christmas meeting with Gordon in Belfast.

Gordon was defended by prominent Belfast solicitor Albert Walmsley who objected to Desmond Curran's use of notes of that conversation. That was because Walmsley had good reason to believe that Desmond's statement contained lies. Permitting him to consult his notes reduced the chances of catching him out in cross-examination. The magistrate, Dr. Mills, ruled that Desmond Curran could refer to them, and court reporters noted that he did so extensively.

The following day Walmsley was on his feet again to object to prosecution evidence being given in open court

Figure 4: Gordon (right) arriving in court for a remand hearing in January 1953.

which he said would prejudice Gordon's chances of a fair trial. The magistrate agreed and the press and the public had to leave the Royal Legion Hall while the disputed evidence – the confession – was heard. Much of the rest of the evidence was heard *in camera*, and on Friday, 6 February, Dr. Mills sent Gordon forward for trial. As he did so, cheering broke out in the public gallery and the magistrate told the police to take the names of three women who had cheered.

The arrest of Gordon for the murder of Patricia Curran on 15 January 1953 ended what was left of the friendship between her brother and Iain Gordon. Had they really been friends, rather than two men tied together by an embarrassing secret? But there was more to it. If Gordon had not 'confessed' to Capstick, suspicion would have continued to fall on members of the Curran family, Desmond included. Iain Gordon probably didn't yet fully understand how Curran's conversations with Detective-Sergeant Deveney had led to his ordeal.

Curran made a further statement to his friend Samuel Deveney on 28 February 1953. The first paragraph is significant because he says that his contact with Gordon had begun earlier than was subsequently made clear to the jury. 'I am a barrister at law, and I reside at the above address [in south Belfast] with my parents. I know Iain H. Gordon from about the end of 1951.'

The rest of the one-page statement lists his three letters from Gordon and the dates on which they were received. These were the letters that Gordon had asked Curran to destroy after reading them. It also lists letters from Gordon to his father, shown to Desmond Curran by Deveney on the pretext that he could verify that they were in Gordon's handwriting.

Why would Deveney ask one possible suspect in a murder investigation to identify the handwriting of another suspect, especially when plenty of independent witnesses, including RAF officers at Edenmore for whom Gordon worked as a filing clerk, could have identified his handwriting? Hawkins had already seen Iain's letters to his father in November 1952 telling him about the murder and about being questioned by the RUC. Additionally, Douglas Gordon had handed over four letters from his son to the police on 17 January 1953, after Iain had been charged with murder, according to sworn evidence at the trial. Deveney showed the letters to Curran to show him what Gordon was saying about their relationship. And there has to be a question over how much more of what would become the prosecution case against Gordon Deveney disclosed to Desmond Curran.

CHAPTER 2

The truth, the whole truth and nothing but the truth

The trial of Iain Hay Gordon for the murder of Patricia Curran began in Belfast on Monday, 2 March 1953, less than four months after her death. That a singularly nasty murder investigation, involving questioning thousands of potential witnesses had been made ready for trial in such a short period was a tribute to the resolve and diligence of the police and the prosecution lawyers, and must have offered some comfort to the public still shocked by the brutality of the murder. Northern Ireland was seen as a legal backwater, and the speed with which those responsible for law and order had brought the matter to this stage of resolution was commendable.

That was made all the more remarkable because it almost coincided with another major legal event: the opening of the inquiry into the sinking of the *Princess Victoria* ferry on the 20-mile voyage from Stranraer in Scotland to Larne in County Antrim. The *Princess Victoria* was a fine modern ship by the standards of the day. One of the world's first roll-on-roll-off ferries, she had been built in Dumbarton, Scotland in 1947, could hold 1,500 passengers, 40 cars and 70 tons of other cargo. When she went down in a gale on the afternoon of 31 January 1953, the stern doors had been breached and water had entered the car decks. Amazingly, despite battling though mountainous waves in what was described as the worst storm in living memory, the stricken ship almost made it from its home port of Stranraer to the mouth of Belfast Lough. Then at 2pm, the captain, James Ferguson, sent out his last message: 'Starboard engine flooded. Ship on her beam ends. Preparing to abandon.' At 2.30pm, the *Princess Victoria* sank.

There were 133 deaths, including Northern Ireland's deputy prime minister Maynard Sinclair, and Sir Walter Smiles[2], MP for North Down. Among the passengers, all the women and children were lost. So too were many senior crew members who had stayed on the stricken ship trying to save it. The disaster was all the more shocking because it involved a routine short crossing in what were believed to be safe and sheltered waters between Northern Ireland and Scotland.

Northern Ireland's Lord Chief Justice John McDermott was about to commence what was probably the most demanding period of his legal career. He was responsible for the complex public inquiry into the sinking of the *Princess Victoria*, due to begin in Belfast on 23 March 1953. But as chief justice, he also felt obliged to take on the trial of Iain Hay Gordon, charged with the murder of his colleague Judge Lance Curran's daughter. McDermott knew the Currans socially; his son John had been at Cambridge with Desmond Curran. It probably would have been impossible to find a judge who didn't know Lance Curran, so small was the membership of the Northern Ireland Bar. The question of obtaining a judge from England or Wales did not arise, it seems, though the RUC had had no compunction in enlisting help from Scotland Yard. Dublin, a hundred miles down the road, was out of the question, though there were competent judges with pre-1922 experience.

---

[2] The explorer Bear Grylls is a great grandson of Walter Smiles.

The legal team for the prosecution was led by Edmond Warnock QC, Northern Ireland's attorney general, with George Hanna QC MP, and Bradley McCall QC in support. Warnock's legal and political career had followed a similar pattern to that of Lance Curran, law and politics, becoming a minister in the Stormont government before becoming attorney general. A clever and resourceful man, he had nonetheless blotted his copybook in 1939 when he told the Northern Ireland cabinet that it was unlikely that German bombers would fly 1,000 miles to attack Belfast. He was then a junior minister in the Home Affairs ministry. Politicians sometimes say silly things, but Warnock's department then neglected its duty to take measures to protect Northern Ireland from air strikes. On Easter Tuesday, 15 April 1941, the Luftwaffe struck. Some 900 people in Belfast died and 1,500 were injured.

Bertie McVeigh QC led for the defence. He had the reputation of being a formidable and tenacious advocate. Like other barristers in this case, he knew the Curran family socially. He had played golf with Lance Curran. In fact, in agreeing to represent Gordon, he had stipulated that he personally would not cross-examine any member of the Curran family. He told Gordon's parents before the trial began that he would prefer to do anything else other than defend their son in this particular case. But it was his duty as a barrister, and he would do it to the best of his ability. The other members of the defence team were John Agnew QC and Basil Kelly. Gordon afterwards said he disliked his legal team, particularly his solicitor Walmsley and that, in his view, Agnew was the best of a bad bunch.

For Monday's *Belfast Telegraph*, the big news was happening at the County Antrim Spring Assizes at Crumlin Road. There was huge public interest in the case. People had begun to queue for places in the public gallery at 8am: standing for two hours in the morning mist and rain. In an evening newspaper, which the *Telegraph* then was, a big problem was that the morning session was taken up with swearing in a jury and other formalities, and the evidence did not begin until mid-afternoon. 'Court crowded for Gordon trial' proclaimed a page one banner headline, and the *Telegraph* marvelled that an unprecedented 35 seats had been provided in the press gallery, including one for a writer from a New York crime magazine.

For a full account of what unfolded at the first day of the trial, the curious had to wait for the next day's morning papers: the *Belfast Newsletter*, the *Northern Whig* and the *Irish News*.

It was almost 4pm before the attorney general of Northern Ireland began setting out the case against Gordon who pleaded not guilty to the charge of murdering Patricia Curran on 12 November 1952. Warnock began by describing the finding of a body in the shrubbery close to her family home in the early hours of the morning. Patricia Curran had caught the 5pm bus home from Belfast and was seen by a boy delivering newspapers to Glen House and Glenavna at the entrance to the drive towards her family home around 5.20pm, he said. Warnock pointed out that Gordon had found it difficult to establish an alibi between 5pm and 6pm on that day and he mentioned Gordon's efforts to get his RAF colleagues to give him one.

Warnock told the jury that there had been a 'violent attack on this girl's virtue, her knickers were torn and bloodstained, and you will come to the conclusion that a determined effort had been made by the assailant to remove her knickers. It would seem that she put up a stern resistance.' Warnock had no factual basis for saying that the attack was sexual in intent. The medical evidence would show that Patricia Curran was a virgin when she died, and not one shred of evidence was produced, then or later, to show that the attack had been sexual. She had, however, put up a struggle, as might be expected of a fit and healthy young woman under attack.

At one point, when it seemed likely that Warnock was going to mention that Gordon had confessed to the murder, Bertie McVeigh interrupted him, and Warnock desisted.

The attorney general wound up his hour-long opening address by saying: 'More than 40,000 people were interviewed in connection with this inquiry, 9,000 statements in writing were taken by the police, the inquiries ranged nationwide and further, and the Crown will seek to convince you that here we are at the end of the quest. Gentlemen, the Crown suggests that the accused was never, at any material time, more than six to seven hundred yards from the scene of the murder.'

The first witness called that afternoon was Head Constable James Cochrane. He was questioned about a map he had made showing the village of Whiteabbey, and the approach to Glen House, home of the Curran family. The prosecution was using his evidence to familiarise the jury with the lie of the land around Glen House and its neighbours. Cochrane produced a map showing the position of the Curran residence at the top of the glen, and how it was approached via gates on Shore Road, part of the main Belfast-Carrickfergus highway along the northern shore of Belfast Lough.

The avenue leading to Glen House was about 600 yards long, Cochrane said, with a fork to the right about 200 yards up the avenue leading to Glenavna, home of Unionist politician Sir Wilson Hungerford. Cochrane had also measured the distance from the Glen House gate lodge to the RAF base at Edenmore at just under half a mile.

Cochrane was also asked about his visit to the avenue at around 5am on 13 November 1952, in the company of Inspector Kennedy and other police. The body had been found in undergrowth about 40 feet in on the left-hand side of the avenue, 50 or 60 yards after the fork, and Patricia Curran's books, handbag and other items lay close to the grass verge of the avenue nearest to where the body was found. Her portfolio and yellow beret were on the ground about one foot from the edge of the avenue. Her handbag had been found two feet three inches from the edge of the avenue. The word portfolio was used in the trial to describe a folder with a hard cover in which Patricia had placed some books, notebooks and letters. When it was found, a ribbon that normally would be used to keep it closed, was missing. Cochrane also described where Patricia Curran's shoes and a glove and buttons were found farther into the undergrowth.

McVeigh had just begun to cross-examine Cochrane when Gordon asked to speak to his solicitor. This done, McVeigh continued to ask about the line of sight in the avenue and the location of streetlamps on Shore Road, and what could be seen through the trees. Not much was the answer. In fact, they were gaslights and not very effective anyway. The RUC man agreed with McVeigh's suggestion that Patricia Curran's portfolio had been deliberately placed on the grass rather than having just fallen there. Cochrane also agreed that there was evidence to suggest that a body had been dragged along the ground at that site.

The second witness was Sergeant Walter Adams, a member of the RUC fingerprints department. He gave evidence of photographing the body in Patricia Curran's family doctor's surgery, and later in the hospital morgue. He had also photographed the site where the body was found, and parts of the nearby village of Whiteabbey. In cross-examination, John Agnew for the defence, asked Adams about a stump, or a twig seen protruding from the ground near where the body was found, but at this remove it is hard to see what point was being made. Cochrane and Adams were the only witnesses heard on the first day of the trial. As it was just 6pm, the judge adjourned proceedings for the day.

Tuesday 3 March 1953

On the second day of the trial, the pace picked up. However, that morning's *Belfast Newsletter* filled the previous day's news gap by highlighting the fact that Dr Rossiter Lewis, a consultant psychiatrist celebrated for his use of a 'lie detector' in high profile cases, would appear for the defence later in the trial.

When proceedings resumed at 10.30 am, the first prosecution witnesses were called to show that Patricia Curran had caught the 5pm bus to Whiteabbey on 12 November. John Steele, an accountancy student who was said to be Patricia's friend but not her boyfriend, told the attorney general that he was eighteen years of age and had got to know Patricia a month earlier. Since then, they had met for coffee about once a week. On the morning in question, he had seen her outside Erskine Mayne's bookshop in Donegall Square West, Belfast and they had arranged to meet again that afternoon for coffee. Afterwards he had escorted her to Smithfield bus station where she had got on the bus to Whiteabbey. He had seen her go upstairs and sit down, and she was alone.

This was confirmed by another passenger on that bus, David Cameron. Patricia Curran had sat alone upstairs and left the bus at Whiteabbey post office at about 5.20pm, he said.

The next witness was a boy aged twelve who initially had difficulty making himself heard in the courtroom. After the judge had asked George Chambers if he understood the importance of telling the truth, the boy was sworn in. He lived at Millmount Cottages, Jordanstown, and he attended Whiteabbey primary school, he told the attorney general. 'I get out of school at half-past-four', George said to Edmond Warnock.

He went home to drop off his schoolbag and then walked to Morrison's shop in Whiteabbey village at 5.10pm for his evening newspaper round. He was waiting for the bus bringing the bundle of papers from Belfast. At 5.20pm, a bus arrived, and he saw Miss Curran get off it, alone, and walk in the direction of the gate to her family home, a distance of about a hundred yards. A few minutes later another bus arrived, bringing his parcel of newspapers.

Soon after half past five, George Chambers set off on his delivery round. He was walking up the drive to Glen House to deliver the evening paper when he heard a factory siren sounding. This meant that it was 5.45pm. He had heard some noises on his way up the drive, but they were leaves rustling and birds singing, and he was quite used to that.

On his way back down the drive, it was pitch black. He had a torch, but when he thought he heard 'somebody's footstep in the leaves', he took fright, and ran the rest of the way down to the main road. George Chambers said he had never been scared before in that driveway like this, even on very dark winter evenings.

Cross-examined by Basil Kelly for the defence, the boy had very little to add, but he insisted that while he had seen Patricia Curran leave the bus and walk alone as far as the gate, he had not seen her turn to go up the drive leading to Glen House. This ended the boy's evidence. The young witness had been gently handled by the judge and counsel for the prosecution and the defence.

Another phase of the prosecution case against Iain Hay Gordon began with the swearing in of a sergeant in the special investigations branch of the RAF's internal police force, William Leathem, who was stationed at Edenmore. The purpose of calling this witness was to show that Gordon had tried and failed to manufacture an alibi for the evening of 12 November, when the prosecution maintained he had murdered Patricia Curran.

In reply to George Hanna for the prosecution, Leathem said that he had visited the grounds of Glen House on the day the body was found. On his return to Edenmore, he had interviewed the airmen who had been present at the base the previous night. He said his focus then was on who had been where between 11pm and midnight the previous night.

Q. 'What did Gordon tell you?'

A. 'He said he was in his billet between 11pm and midnight.'

At this point the judge became irritated by the behaviour of some spectators in the court. 'Will people stop whispering please at the back? In this court it is very difficult sometimes to hear, and it is particularly [so] when people are whispering at the back. Please keep quiet while the witness is giving evidence.'

According to Leathem, Gordon had left the room at the end of the interview and had returned 15 minutes later. No reason was given in evidence for this absence. It appeared that when the interview ended, Gordon had second thoughts, and then went back to volunteer the information that in the past he had visited the Curran house and met Patricia. Leathem was not questioned on this point however, and the judge appeared to have been still distracted by the whispering in court.

The prosecution questioning continued.

Q. 'Did he say anything to you then?'

A. 'He volunteered the information that he knew the deceased girl and her family.'

Q. 'Did he say anything else?'

A. 'Gordon said he had met the family, he had met her brother Desmond several times previously when leaving church and had been invited to the Curran home several times, the last time being about three months previously. At the Curran home, he had met Patricia Curran. He knew her as a very athletic and a very pleasant girl. But that was all. He thought he had better come back and tell us. He said he didn't know whether the information would be of use to us or not, but he thought he had better come back and tell us.'

Sergeant Leathem said that as a result of information received – which he did not explain – his focus had shifted to the period between five and six pm of the evening before the body was found. He spoke to Gordon again on the evening of 14 November 1952.

George Hanna took up the questioning.

Q. 'What did he say on that occasion?'

A. 'I asked him to account for his movements. He said he had been in Whiteabbey post office at 4.30pm. After leaving the post office he returned to Edenmore, was in the dining hall from five o'clock until ten past, walked the short distance from the dining hall to the billet [sleeping quarters] with Corporal [Henry] Connor; remained in the billet for some time. But how the time was spent, he wasn't sure whether he was reading or writing. After that, he went to the main building, up to the office, where he worked, and remained there for some time and went down to the NAAFI for a cup of tea after it opened.'

Three days later, Sergeant Leathem said, he took Gordon to the RUC barracks at Whiteabbey.

Q. 'Did you see Sergeant Black of the RUC taking a statement in writing from Gordon?'

A. 'I saw Gordon writing out a statement on that occasion, my Lord.'

This exchange is significant. Leathem, a military police sergeant, is making a clear distinction between his RUC counterpart, Sergeant Black, obtaining a written statement from Gordon, as opposed to recording Gordon's answers to questions and getting him to sign them. It also points to Gordon's own preference for writing things down.

Having returned with Gordon to RAF Edenmore, Leathem said he escorted Corporal Henry Connor to Whiteabbey RUC station to be interviewed. Connor was the RAF man whom Gordon named as being present in the NAAFI on the afternoon of 12 November, and with whom he said he had walked to his billet at 5.10pm. Sergeant Black interviewed Connor and following that Leathem returned again to Edenmore. There he, Gordon and Connor walked the path from the NAAFI to the billets where the men had their sleeping quarters.

'The accused pointed out a place where the path forked and said that was where he parted from Corporal Connor on the night of the murder', Leathem told prosecuting counsel. Leathem had then gone into the billets and asked if anyone present recalled seeing Gordon there or thereabouts between 5 and 6pm on the evening in question. No one had. Gordon was present when Leathem put that question, he said.

In cross-examination by Bertie McVeigh for the defence, the military police sergeant agreed that on 13 November he had been questioning RAF personnel about where they were between 11pm and midnight. On the next day, his focus had shifted to the time between 5 and 6 pm. He confirmed that three days later he brought Gordon to Whiteabbey temporary police station where he gave a written statement to Sergeant Black, the RUC officer in charge, and he, Leathem, confirmed that he had not obtained a written statement from Gordon before that.

The next witness was Sergeant William Black who confirmed that Gordon had written the following statement for him on 17 November 1953, at Whiteabbey police station:

> I remember 12 November 1952. I was taking the official mail down to Whiteabbey post office between four and four thirty pm. After leaving the post office, I went up to Quiery's [shop] to collect any newspapers for RAF Edenmore. Whereupon I returned to camp and stayed in camp the rest of the evening. I was not out at all. I was in the central registry [the office in which Gordon worked during the day; elsewhere he said he went there after hours to write letters

and practice typing] from about six thirty pm till nine pm, with one visit to the NAAFI roughly between seven thirty and eight pm. I went to bed about between nine thirty and ten pm.

I knew Desmond Curran best of all the Currans. He spoke to me after coming out of church and would accompany me as far as the Manse Road on my way back to camp. The first Sunday he spoke to me, he invited me to their home for dinner. I was there on three other occasions, perhaps. I met all the family: Justice Curran, Mrs Curran, Michael, Desmond and Patricia. I also think that Michael's girl [friend] was there as well on the first visit to the house. I don't think Patricia was there. I believe her mother stated that she had stayed the night with one of her chums and would return later. I never saw her on that occasion but did on the other occasions. I know very little about Patricia and absolutely nothing about her private life. She struck me as being very intelligent, full of life and the last person anyone would want to harm.

Desmond never spoke about the other members of his family or mentioned anything appertaining to them. Patricia Curran never talked about what she had been doing during the short time that I did see her. I saw her just before I left them. I had a cup of tea with them. The black eye I have was caused on the Sunday prior to the murder. It happened in the billet and was more of an accident than anything else … Hynes or someone else I was 'scrapping' with at the time.

Iain Hay Gordon

Questioned by the attorney general, William Black said that having read Gordon's statement he asked him to account for his movements between 5 and 6 pm on 12 November.

'Gordon had replied: "I was having my tea at five pm with Corporal Connor. We both left the mess [NAAFI] and walked towards our billets … separated before we reached our billets … I then had a wash".'

In reply to the judge, Sergeant Black said that he had initially intended to question Gordon and write down his answers to questions he put to him. But he had unexpectedly been called away and, in his absence, Gordon had begun to write, and later answered supplementary questions.

The next witness to be called gave testimony that pushed the unfolding narrative forward by almost a fortnight. RUC Detective Sergeant Samuel Jeffrey gave evidence of interviewing Gordon at RAF Edenmore, accompanied by Detective Sergeant Denis Hawkins of Scotland Yard, on 29 November 1952. The attorney general – in opening the prosecution case to the jury the previous day – had mentioned the two London detectives, but had largely left their presence unexplained. The jury was expected to fill in the blanks.

Jeffrey said that on 29 November 1952 Hawkins had told Gordon that they were not satisfied with the explanation he had given Sergeant Black in his statement of 17 November. He had further questions for him about his movements on the afternoon of 12 November.

Gordon's reply repeated what he had told Sergeant Black with the addition of some detail. When he had gone to the central registry, it was to practice his typing for a forthcoming examination. The interview lasted about 25 minutes, Jeffrey said. Then Sergeant Hawkins asked Gordon to take him to see the places he had mentioned: the billets, the NAAFI and the central registry. This was done, and while at the billets Gordon had shown the two sergeants the 'civvies' he had changed into after work that day, a sports-coat and flannels. They had examined the garments but had found nothing of interest.

McVeigh cross-examined for the defence. He asked Jeffrey if he had a copy of Gordon's statement to Sergeant Black during his own interview. Jeffrey said he had not, and his interest was in Gordon's movements, rather than his earlier statement about them. Jeffrey admitted that Gordon had 'adhered' to his earlier statement. He denied that there was a difference between 'an interview' and 'questioning' as far as he was concerned. He was unaware that Gordon had already been questioned twice about his movements, and thus did not know that by the time he and Hawkins got to question Gordon on 29 November, it was the fourth time he had been asked to account for his movements.

Albert Davidson was then sworn in. 'You're a detective-constable in the Royal Ulster Constabulary stationed at Glengormley?' [Glengormley is about four miles from Whiteabbey.]

'I am, my lord.'

Davidson gave evidence of being sent to Dr Wilson's surgery at Whiteabbey at 5.15am on 13 November, and taking charge of the body of Patricia Curran until he was relieved at 9.05 am. He then went to assist in taking measurements at the scene where the body had been found. He had observed a 'trail mark' on the ground. 'It started at the point where the shoes had been found. It is marked on the map [given in evidence], continued around the tree trunk and ended up near the tree at the upper side of the map.'

Davidson testified that he had found a brooch and a colleague had found a button; both had been handed to Detective Sergeant Deveney for safekeeping. Samuel Deveney appears often in this narrative; in his first appearance, chronologically speaking, he is the RUC officer in charge of collating evidence at the place where the body was found.

On 4 December 1952, Constable Davidson had spoken to Iain Gordon at RAF Edenmore. 'I told him I was making a check of the movements of all men at Edenmore on the evening of November 12, 1952, the date of the murder of Miss Patricia Curran.' Since Gordon replied in the same terms as he had done on the previous occasions, there is no need to repeat that information here. Capstick would question him again in mid-December but took no notes. Gordon's answers remained consistent throughout until 14 January 1953.

Under cross-examination by Basil Kelly who was assisting Bertie McVeigh and John Agnew for the defence, Davidson agreed that, despite the intensive search carried out at the scene where the body was found, nothing turned up that could – in any way be – be connected to Iain Gordon. He agreed that the trail mark he had seen suggested that the body had been dragged a distance of about 40 feet. And he denied any knowledge of a press conference or police statement to the press four days after the body had been found which claimed that there was no evidence of any dragging of the body at the scene.

There were three more witnesses before lunch.

Mrs. Mary Jackson, wife of Wing Commander Bill Jackson, a senior officer at RAF Edenmore, took the stand. 'Wearing a high fez-shaped white hat', according to reporters present who showed very little interest in what other witnesses wore, she told the court she had no doubt that she had seen Gordon going down the drive of Edenmore as she was returning from shopping in the village on the evening of the murder. This was at 5.10pm, she said, and she had passed Gordon on her bicycle. She could not recall if he was wearing a uniform or not, she told Bertie McVeigh in cross-examination. Try as he might, he was unable to shake her testimony. Brenda Gordon, Iain's mother, thought Mrs. Jackson was over-dressed for a court hearing and 'playing to the gallery' as she gave evidence.

Mrs. Jackson was followed into the witness box by Corporal Henry Connor who appeared surprised to be initially asked about events on 13 November by prosecution counsel. He recalled being at tea in the mess hall at Edenmore with two colleagues, one called Spence, the other whose name has been redacted in the court record. On the following day, 14 November, Connor said that Gordon had asked him to say– if asked by the RAF police – that they had had tea together in the mess at 5pm on the day of the murder. Gordon also asked him to say that they had walked together towards the billets, afterwards until the path forked, where they had parted company.

The next questions that Edmond Warnock put to Connor were crucial:

Q. 'In fact, did you have tea with Gordon on the afternoon of 12 November?'

A. 'No sir, I didn't.'

Q. 'Did you see Gordon between five and half-past-six on 12 November at all?'

A. 'No, sir.'

In cross-examination, John Agnew for the defence tried to mend some fences, but in vain. Connor denied that he and others had been warned to have their stories straight about their movements on 12 November before the military police began asking questions.

Connor's performance in the witness box was not impressive. He was on a sticky wicket to begin with, because at the very least he was admitting to wasting police time by providing Gordon with a false alibi. He became flustered when asked about whom he had given statements to, and he contradicted himself over being warned about what he had said to the military police. The police had at one stage suggested to Connor that rather than Gordon asking him to provide an alibi, it was the other way around, and he had sought Gordon's support. However, his testimony on not seeing Gordon on the afternoon of the murder remained unshaken.

There was one more witness before lunch. Irene Crawford, a counter assistant at RAF Edenmore. She recalled Gordon being at the NAAFI at around 7pm on 12 November. He was alone. He ordered a cup of tea.

'Can you say how he was dressed?'

'Sir, he had a Dexter on and a blue scarf.' [A Dexter appears to be a brand of tee-shirt.]

'Was he in civilian clothes?'

'Yes.'

The following morning, she said, Gordon had come to the NAAFI when it was closed between breaks and asked her to confirm that he had been there the previous night. She had replied that she wasn't daft. And he had gone away.

When the jury returned after lunch, Judge McDermott explained to them that the defence had raised the question of the admissibility of the evidence they were just about to hear from a series of witnesses. He asked the jury to retire while the court considered that matter, and he would summon them when it had been resolved. So, five minutes after returning from lunch, the jury was sent away again, while a *voir dire* took place; a 'trial within a trial,' in which the judge decided if disputed evidence was admissible in the main proceedings.

In the absence of the jury, RUC Constable Charlton Herdman took the stand. But before his evidence began, Bertie McVeigh objected to the sequence in which the witnesses were to be presented. Herdman was about to give evidence out of chronological order, and the picture unfolding was thus being made difficult for the jury to follow. The judge said the order of prosecution witnesses was a matter for the prosecution, and he would hear all the challenged testimony together. With hindsight, the judge would have been advised to heed McVeigh on this point. McDermott was driving this trial too quickly, not allowing lawyers and jury members sufficient time to absorb what they were seeing and hearing.

In response to questions from George Hanna for the prosecution, Constable Herdman said he was in charge of the RUC escort which accompanied Gordon to Whiteabbey Petty Sessions on 5 February 1953. He was sitting on one side of the accused in court when depositions were being taken, with another constable on the other side. The pathologist, Dr. Wells, was giving evidence when a knife was produced in evidence. Gordon was watching proceedings intently, he said. The knife was handed to the magistrate Dr. Mills, but it unexpectedly fell to the courtroom floor,

Herdman said: 'The accused turned to me and said: "That's not it." I was surprised and said 'Why?'. He [Gordon] then added – "That is the ordinary kind of service knife as issued and used in the office – the one I had had a longer blade – sure they haven't found it yet'.

Herdman went on to say that Gordon was still looking at the knife as he continued speaking. 'I believe Miss Curran carried one in her handbag.'

The attorney general: 'Constable, did you say anything to cause or encourage the accused to speak to you?'

Herdman: 'I did not, my lord'

In cross-examination, McVeigh tried to get Herdman to admit that he had prompted or encouraged Gordon to speak, but the RUC man insisted that the only word he said was 'Why?' and he had uttered that word involuntarily.

McVeigh did get Herdman to admit that when he made a deposition about this exchange, his question 'Why?' had been left out. McVeigh was making the point that when

Gordon began making potentially damaging admissions, Herdman, a policeman, should have cautioned him rather than asking questions and so encouraging him to continue. Herdman rejected this, saying Gordon had spoken so quickly, he had no time to caution him.

Judge McDermott was taking a close interest in this exchange and intervened with clarifying questions. Yet Herdman's remarkable assertion that Gordon said that Patricia Curran habitually carried a knife in her handbag which was capable of being used to murder her was not addressed. How could Gordon know this? Why didn't the judge – who routinely intervened on less substantial matters – pursue this point? Why didn't the defence do so? In denying that this was the right knife, was Gordon suggesting that another knife was the 'right knife', and what did this mean for his defence?

Detective Sergeant Denis Hawkins was called. He said he was a member of the staff at Scotland Yard. He agreed that he was 'assisting in the investigation into the Curran murder', as the attorney general put it to him.

First, Hawkins confirmed, in so many words, Detective Sergeant Jeffrey's account of the interview they had conducted with Gordon at Edenmore on 29 November: 'I told Gordon that I was not satisfied with his previous explanation [of his movements on the day of the murder].' Hawkins had taken a statement from Gordon and went with him to see for himself where Gordon had been that evening.

Warnock moved on to questioning Hawkins about his formal interview of Iain Gordon. Hawkins had told Gordon to present himself at the temporary RUC barracks at Edenmore at 10 am on 13 January 1953. This would be the first day of what the defence argued was a three-day police assault on Gordon's refusal to admit that he had murdered the nineteen-year-old student.

Hawkins: 'I told him I wanted to talk to him about his family, his background, his habits and his relationship with the family of Mr. Justice Curran.'

Warnock: 'And did you make any suggestion to him?'

Hawkins: 'I said that, if he liked, he could have a RAF officer present and I would arrange it.'

At the time of these interviews, Gordon was not yet twenty-one years old, and was thus a 'child' in the eyes of the law. He was entitled to have a parent or guardian present when the police were questioning him. Had an RAF officer been present at the interviews, he/she would be expected to insist that Gordon would be cautioned against incriminating himself if the questioning looked likely to lead to him being charged with a criminal offence.

Gordon declined to have an RAF officer present, according to Hawkins. 'From 10 o'clock, my Lord, I had a general conversation with the accused until about 11am. I then started taking a statement from him, in answer to my questions, and writing it down.'

At this point it is worth noting that Hawkins had been alone with Gordon for 90 minutes that morning. Hawkins said that he began to take down Gordon's statement at about 11am. Head Constable Russell joined them half an hour later and he continued writing down Gordon's statement. They broke for lunch at 12.15pm, Hawkins said.

The questioning and statement-taking resumed at 3pm, with Russell still present, according to Hawkins. In response to the attorney general, Hawkins said that he had not questioned Gordon about his movements on the day of the murder during this, the first day of the three-day interrogation. The judge restated the question, and Hawkins confirmed that neither the murder, nor Gordon's account of his movements on the day of the murder, were mentioned in the course of the 13 January interrogation. So, a man who was a suspect in a murder investigation spent practically the whole of one working day, Tuesday 13 January, being closely questioned, but not about the murder nor about his alibi, according to the sworn evidence of Detective Sergeant Denis Hawkins of Scotland Yard.

The attorney general then read to the court Hawkins's account of what Gordon had said to him and Head Constable Russell. In it, Gordon gave an extended retelling of his first dealings with the Curran family. He began by describing meeting Desmond Curran in October 1951:

> He spoke to me as I left church one Sunday. He told me his name and started discussing religious topics. After some conversation, he invited me home for lunch. We walked by some back way, I believe up the Manse Road, and across some fields. When we got there, he introduced me to his father and mother and brother Michael.
>
> Patricia was not there that Sunday. The family appeared fairly pleased to see me. I used to see Desmond every Sunday. I went [to Glen House] on three other occasions.

Gordon had gone on to provide further detail on his interactions with Desmond Curran:

> Desmond was the only one [of the family] interested in Moral Re-Armament, as far as I knew. About six weeks before Patricia was murdered, I borrowed a pound from Desmond to pay for shoe repairs. I repaid this money to him about the middle of December [1952]. I did not tell him that I met him specifically to repay the money. I previously asked the Reverend Wylie if there was any objection to me meeting Desmond. [Wylie was the Presbyterian minister in Whiteabbey who had introduced Iain Hay Gordon to Desmond Curran and was on friendly terms with both men.]

While I was with Desmond, I told him
that Wesley Courtney [a barber in nearby
Newtownabbey] had made an immoral advance
to me. I told Desmond that I had rejected the
advance. We spoke about homosexuality. I have
no inclination that way, and as far as I know
neither has Desmond. I still continue to be
friendly with Desmond.

The first day of this round of questioning concluded
at about 4.30pm, according to Hawkins, who said initially
that it ended at 4pm then changed that to 4.30pm. Gordon
maintained that it went on longer. Gordon was told to return
the following day, 14 January, when Hawkins and Russell
would resume questioning him and his statement would be
concluded.

On the following morning, the focus of the resumed
interrogation turned to Gordon's alibi. Gordon, according to
Hawkins, paused for some minutes then said:

I want to tell you the truth about what
happened on Wednesday night [the night of
the murder]. On Thursday 13th at about 5.05 or
5.10 pm, I was having my tea in the dining hall
at Edenmore. The dining hall was full. One of
the NCOs – I believe it was Sergeant Maxey
– shouted from the doorway something like:
'Arrange between yourselves who you were with
between five and six last night.' The sergeant said
we were to report together to the RAF police.
Corporal Connor came to me and said: 'You say
you were sitting with me.' He gave me no reason
for saying this, it might have been because he
was sitting on his own at that time. We were
fairly friendly though he was an NCO.'

I said to Connor: 'I cannot say that, because
I went straight to central registry after the tea.'

Another airman who was passing – it might have been Davidson – said: 'It won't matter.' I had serious misgivings about it, but did, in fact, agree to tell the RAF police a lying story. It was a lie because I was not with Connor that Wednesday evening. We both went to the RAF police and told them the same story [about having tea together in the dining hall and then walking over to the billet]. I was in the central registry that night, and I was alone.

Everything else I told you about what happened before 5pm is the truth … when I left the dining hall I went straight to central registry. I was in RAF uniform. I left central registry between 7 and 7.30pm. I may have gone to the billet and changed into civilian clothes before I went to the NAAFI. I returned to the registry and continued my typing until 9.30pm.

Hawkins's examination concluded with him telling the attorney general about the morning of 15 January 1953, when Gordon presented himself at the temporary RUC barracks at 9.30am. This was the third consecutive day of the interrogation. Hawkins said that Gordon was by then aware that he was to be questioned by John Capstick of Scotland Yard, to whom Hawkins reported.

McVeigh then cross-examined Hawkins. The initial exchange is worth quoting in full because a sloppiness about recording dates is becoming evident: 'Sergeant Hawkins on 17, 29 [sic] of November, you had questioned the accused. Isn't that correct?'

Hawkins: 'It is correct, sir.'

McVeigh: 'Yes, now was 29 November the first time you had seen the accused?' Hawkins had just agreed that he had seen Gordon on the 17 November.

Hawkins: 'Yes, sir, yes.'

McVeigh: 'Did you know at that time [29 November 1952] that he was by way of being odd, peculiar?'

Hawkins: 'I knew nothing peculiar about him, sir, only the impression I formed.'

Hawkins went on to say that he could not decide what to make of Iain Hay Gordon, one way or the other. He admitted he had known that Gordon was under twenty-one years of age. He had contacted the Edenmore camp commander, Pilot Officer Richard Popple, who had made it clear that an RAF officer should be present if a written statement was being taken. Hawkins told the defence counsel he had chosen to ignore what Popple had said to him about having an RAF officer present when a written statement was being taken.

McVeigh took Hawkins back to 13 January, the first of the three days of interrogation. Why had Hawkins been questioning Gordon for more than hour on that morning before Head Constable Russell joined them?

Hawkins: 'I wanted to get an impression of the lad and know what he was like.' Hawkins said he had guided the conversation, but gave no specifics about what was discussed, apart from saying he had asked Gordon about his family, his early life, school, and how he was getting on in the RAF.

After Russell joined Hawkins, both men had questioned Gordon together.

McVeigh: 'Was there anyone else present during all that [first] day – 13 January?'

Hawkins: 'Somebody may have walked in for a minute, but as regards the interview, no-one else was present.'

McVeigh: 'Was Inspector Kennedy or Superintendent Capstick present on the afternoon of 13 January at any time?"

Hawkins: 'I'm sure they were not. They were in the building but not in the room.'

McVeigh: 'Who asked the questions about Gordon's sexual life?'

Hawkins: 'Both Head Constable Russell and myself.'

Hawkins then said he had probably brought up the subject of Gordon's sexual experience first. He asked Gordon about girlfriends. He had done so first before Russell had joined the interrogation, and the subject had been raised again in Russell's presence.

Hawkins could not recall if he or Russell had first asked Gordon about homosexuality, but he admitted that Russell had pressed him on that subject 'but not unduly'. Gordon maintained that Russell had been roaring and shouting at him about this.

In his cross-examination of Hawkins, McVeigh made much of two aspects of that day's questioning of Gordon. One was the length of time spent on questions about sexual matters – in a case where no evidence of any sexual aspect had been put forward – and the second was the degree of pressure applied by the two police officers. McVeigh strongly suggested that it was oppressive; Hawkins insisted that it was not.

On that topic, the judge indicated that he had heard enough.

McVeigh then wanted to know if Hawkins was aware that Capstick had been with Gordon for about ten minutes before the interrogation resumed on the second day of interrogation, 14 January 1953.

Hawkins: 'I think not, sir, because I arrived with Superintendent Capstick. I think it impossible.'

McVeigh: 'Well, did you know that that he [Capstick] said that he saw him [Gordon] on 14 January at 9.50am?' [McVeigh was here quoting from Capstick's deposition at a remand hearing.]

McVeigh invited Hawkins to criticise his superior officer. 'You would be surprised if somebody had attempted to forestall you [in hijacking an interview that you had arranged?]. Would you think that a bit irregular?', he asked the sergeant.

Hawkins's reply was masterly: 'Anybody except my superintendent.'

McVeigh continued to question Hawkins over the conduct of the second consecutive day of interrogation. The first session ran until 1.30pm. Hawkins countered that they had cups of tea but admitted that the questioning had continued practically without a break.

Because lunch service was over in Edenmore, Hawkins said the three men went to a pub called the Crown in Belfast [Gordon said they went to the restaurant at the Royal Courts of Justice] and resumed the interrogation at 3pm. Hawkins and Russell continued to ask questions. Hawkins wrote down the answers. At 4pm, Gordon began to read the notes and initialled each page in turn. This concluded at about 4.30pm. Then Capstick entered the room and began reading Gordon's statement. From the court transcript, it appears that Corporal Connor been sent for and had arrived at the temporary police barracks at about 5pm, and Hawkins left to take a statement in another room from him and another person, whose name has been redacted. (The police had contacted Connor at home that day and told him that Gordon had just admitted that his alibi was a pack of lies and that this made him – Connor – a suspect for the murder of Patricia Curran. Connor was then brought to Whiteabbey for interrogation. The court was led to believe that, at first, Connor had come clean about the alibi but in fact he didn't break until after Gordon did. This was a typical Capstick manoeuvre, Charlie Artful in action.)

McVeigh asked about Gordon's whereabouts at this stage: 'The accused states that the statements of Connor and the other person were brought into the room while he was being questioned by this witness [Hawkins] and Head Constable Russell.'

'Quite wrong, sir', Hawkins replied.

Judge McDermott asked the same question again and got an unequivocal denial from Hawkins, who went to say that he kept Connors's and other statements with him at all times that evening.

McVeigh did manage to extract from Hawkins that in the 30 minutes of conversation he had alone with Gordon on the morning of 15 January, the only topic the policeman could recall being discussed was the weather.

The judge called the mid-afternoon tea break. When proceedings resumed at 4.34pm, Head Constable Samuel Russell was examined for the prosecution by George Hanna.

Hanna: 'Did Sergeant Hawkins take down in writing information which the accused man Gordon gave in answers by you and Hawkins?'

Russell: 'He did, my lord.'

Then Hanna shifted to the third day – after Gordon had confessed and been charged. 'On 15 January of this year, did you take from the accused some items that were in his possession, and did you place them in an envelope?'

Russell: 'Yes, my lord.'

Hanna: 'What time was this?'

Russell: 'About twenty minutes to ten on the night of 15 January.'

Hanna: 'Did you hear some words that he said?'

Russell: 'He said words that I didn't catch, my lord, followed by: "I feel much happier now that I've told the truth".'

Cross-examining for the defence, Basil Kelly tried to get Russell to explain why Gordon had not been cautioned. Russell said that Gordon had spoken before he had had a chance to caution him. Kelly said that a policeman's duty was to be fair to the accused, and that a caution should have been administered when Gordon was charged.

Kelly then turned to Russell's part in the 13 and 14 January interrogation of Gordon and noted that that no caution had been administered on either day.

Russell said he had learned that Gordon was under twenty-one after he had been arrested. (His twenty-first birthday occurred a few days after he had been charged with murder.) Russell said that he had heard Gordon refuse to have an RAF officer present when he was being questioned.

Kelly: 'Do you consider, Head [Constable], that you were being scrupulously fair close questioning a young airman for two days without either a parent or an RAF officer there?'

Russell: 'Yes, I do, my lord.'

The judge intervened and said that that particular question was for him to decide, and he would do so in due course.

Basil Kelly did not press the matter. Instead he asked the head constable how the statement compiled over the two days had been put together. Russell told him it was made up of Gordon's answers to questions, some put by him and others by Sergeant Hawkins. Russell had missed the beginning of the first day's interrogation, and Hawkins had already begun writing the statement when Russell got there at 11.30 am. Russell agreed that he had known that Gordon had been questioned four times already about his movements on the day of the murder. (In fact, five or six times, perhaps more, but it is fair to say that Russell was probably answering for what he knew.)

Russell explained that when he joined Hawkins in the interview room, his intention had been again to bring up the question of Gordon's movements and so obtain the real truth about them, but Hawkins had forestalled him by saying that he was now taking a statement from Gordon about his family background.

The exchange that followed between defence barrister Basil Kelly and RUC head constable Samuel Russell has never been satisfactorily explained:

Kelly: 'Do you agree that the only way that Gordon could have told the truth, as you thought it was the truth, was by breaking down under *[sic]* or by close questioning?'

Russell: 'No, my lord.'

Kelly: 'Or we will put it this way: the only way that Gordon could have changed his story was by an answer made, an answer to your questions?'

Russell: 'No, my lord. if he could have provided me with the names of his relatives when I saw him between 5 and 6pm, I would have been satisfied.'

Since nobody, not the judge, not the attorney general, and not the defence counsel, made any attempt to find out what Russell meant by this, perhaps the record is simply garbled. Did Russell mean to say 'witnesses' instead of 'relatives'?

There followed a scrappy exchange between Kelly and the RUC man over whether Sergeant Hawkins had used the words 'sexual habits', 'masturbation' and 'homosexuality' in questioning Gordon. It emerged that while Hawkins was giving evidence earlier, Russell had been listening in court. That is not allowed today because of the danger that yet-to-be-called witnesses listening in court might 'tailor' evidence to suit what has gone before.

Under cross-examination by Basil Kelly, Russell denied that he had first brought up the subject of Gordon's sexual habits as Hawkins had said in his evidence. Two police witnesses – Russell and Hawkins – gave contradictory sworn evidence on this point.

Basil Kelly then pursued the suggestion that the questioning and pressure on Gordon had continued into the meal breaks,

Russell said that he ran down the road to Whiteabbey RUC station to talk to a detective there during a lunch break on the first day. In doing so, he passed Gordon who had left before him. 'I halted in my running and made some remark to him and passed on, my lord.' Later when Kelly asked Russell about the delayed lunch on the second day, Russell replied that it was quite normal for them to go the law courts building in Belfast for lunch and that he, Hawkins and Gordon gone there that day. Kelly appeared to have missed the confusion over the lunch venue. This was an opportunity to ask if the interrogation continued over lunch without a break, as Gordon claimed.

Russell denied being on his own with Gordon at any time during the afternoon and insisted that neither Kennedy nor Capstick had at any time entered the room where the questioning was taking place on 13 or 14 January. Gordon's whereabouts on the day after the murder were not discussed until late on 14 January after almost two full days of questioning, he said.

A jury – had it been present in court to hear this evidence – might well have had difficulty with the police witnesses saying that long periods of time passed discussing matters that could have been disposed of in a fraction of that time. How much time does a gauche and immature 20-year-old male require to say all there is to say about masturbation to an RUC head constable? Or did an experienced investigator like Hawkins really need thirty minutes face-to-face with Gordon on the subject of the weather? The written record provides no good answers to what happened in the interview room. The defence chose not to call Gordon as a witness, so he was not able to help. Gordon's solicitor Walmsley had been adamant on this point: he was still angry with his client over what he did – or did not – say to Constable Herdman about the 'wrong" knife at an earlier hearing.

When the questioning was over, and Gordon had read and signed the statement, Russell said he left the room as did Hawkins. Kelly extracted from Russell the possibility that Capstick spent 30 minutes alone with Gordon after the statement was signed.

RUC inspector John Nelson was sworn. At 10.10am on 15 January 1953, he had interrupted Hawkins who was questioning Gordon on his own to tell him that he was required on the telephone. When Hawkins left the room, Nelson said that he asked Gordon how he was. Gordon had told him he was unhappy. 'He said it was because he hadn't told the truth about some things. I said it was unwise to tell the police a lot of lies because when he told one lie, he would have to tell another to support it and the lying would go on. He said he realised this ... he then changed the subject and spoke about his early life.'

Later that day, Nelson said that Gordon was arrested, and that he and Head Constable Russell had taken him to Belfast prison. 'After he had been admitted, Gordon turned to him and said: 'I'm glad I took your advice. I feel a lot happier now that I have told the truth.'

Under cross-examination, Nelson stated that the only reason he spent ten minutes alone with Gordon on the morning of the confession was solely due to Hawkins being needed on the phone, and Capstick not having arrived. Nelson insisted that his intervention was not planned, there had been a phone call for Hawkins, and his presence in the interview room was not a contrivance to see if Gordon was amenable to another line of approach.

Nelson said he did not know of the movements of other police that day and could not say if Gordon had been questioned by relays of policemen. His evidence having ended, the attorney general recalled Nelson who again denied that he had gone to Gordon in the morning with the express purpose of interrogating him, rather than his stated purpose of telling Hawkins that there was a phone call for him and staying with Gordon until the call was ended. However, in admitting that he began his conversation with Gordon with a question, Nelson provided further credibility to the defence's contention about 'relays of policemen' subjecting Gordon to continuous forceful interrogation over three days.

Unfortunately, the jury was not present to hear Hawkins and Russell and Nelson defend themselves against this challenge to the official version of police tactics. Nor did the jury hear that Russell and Hawkins gave contradictory accounts of the way in which the subject of Gordon's sexual habits was raised with the accused and what that meant for the credibility of prosecution witnesses.

The effect of the *voir dire* – the trial within a trial ,which would continue into the next day – on the lawyers involved is difficult to gauge. Judge and prosecution and defence lawyers alike now had to hold two versions of the proceedings in their head: that which the jury knew, and that which they knew but the jury did not. Experienced lawyers were expected to handle such difficulties, but in a complex and distressing trial involving the murder of a colleague's daughter, being driven full tilt by a determined chief justice, that wasn't going to be easy. Nor was it.

The court rose at 5.40pm.

Wednesday 4 March 1953

When the court resumed, the jury was sent out again, as the *voir dire* continued. The first witness was Detective Superintendent John Capstick of London's Metropolitan Police. The main topic of Capstick's evidence was the confession that Gordon had made on the afternoon of the third day of questioning.

In reply to Edmond Warnock, Capstick agreed that his job was to assist the RUC's investigation of the murder of

Patricia Curran. He said that on the morning of 15 January 1953, the day Gordon confessed, he had had a 'general conversation' with the accused, just the two of them, covering homosexuality, masturbation and associated matters, lasting two hours and 55 minutes. Although this session lasted for a little under three hours, Capstick took just one short note of about 30 words. He said that the conversation was not about matters which affected the murder investigation. How one could discuss homosexuality and masturbation for so long was not explained. One might have thought that Hawkins and Russell had covered that ground adequately on the previous day. The defence contended that Capstick was piling pressure on Gordon, to break down his resistance and get him to confess to the murder in return for leaving out the sordid details of his homosexual encounters about which he was deeply ashamed and didn't want his parents to know. Besides, homosexuality was then a criminal offence and Gordon could have been forced out of the RAF in disgrace.

After lunch in the barracks interrogation room, for which Capstick and Kennedy were both present, Kennedy left and Capstick and Gordon were alone together yet again. Capstick said he told Gordon to stop telling lies to the police. Gordon had thought about that for a while then asked: 'Did anyone see me leaving the Glen?' Gordon was referring to the wooded area, not Glen House.

Capstick asked him if he was willing take part in an identification parade? Gordon replied: 'I refuse to be put for identification. The Lord and my mother know I can speak the truth and I am now going to do so. I'm very sorry I told you lies about the murder.'

Capstick told Gordon to stop there while he phoned Inspector Kennedy and asked him to return. When Kennedy entered the room, Capstick told him that Gordon was about to tell the truth.

Gordon then said: 'I did it in a black-out.' He was cautioned and then asked that his statement in which he admitted murdering Patricia Curran be written down. After Gordon had completed dictating the statement, but before signing it, Capstick said that Gordon asked for time to consider and Kennedy agreed. Some slight changes were made, and Gordon signed the statement and was charged with murder. 'It was not a wilful murder' he then said, according to Capstick, who had written down the confession.

Warnock, the attorney general, then read Gordon's confession to the court:

I left the camp at Edenmore on Wednesday after-noon, 12 November 1952, to deliver the [camp's outgoing] mail to Whiteabbey post office. I was in there for five to ten minutes, then I went to Quiery's paper shop in the main street to collect the camp newspapers. I would not be very long in there.

I believe I called in at the bookies, approx-imately opposite Quiery's but off the main road. I placed a bet there on a horse for one of the air-men at the camp. I forget his name. I think I then went back to the camp with the newspapers. I probably had my tea about 5pm. It took me about five minutes for my tea. I think I then changed into my civilian wear of sports coat and flannels.

I walked back alone to Whiteabbey and met Patricia Curran [on the Shore Road] between the Glen and Whiteabbey post office.

She said to me 'Hello Iain' or something like that. I said, 'Hello Patricia'. We had a short general conversation. I forget what we talked about, but she asked me to escort her to her home up the Glen. I agreed to do so because it was fairly dark and there was none of the family at the gate to the Glen. I can understand anyone being afraid of going up the Glen in the dark, because the light is completely cut out because the trees meet at the top. I noticed Patricia was carrying a handbag and something else – I just forget what it was. It appeared to be wrapped up whatever it was, books or something.

She was wearing a yellow hat. It was just about [at] the Glen entrance where she first spoke to me. We both walked up the Glen together and I think I was on her left-hand side. After we had walked a few yards, I either held her left hand or arm as we walked along. She did not object and was quite cheerful. We carried on walking up the Glen until we came to the spot where the streetlamp's light does not reach. It was quite dark there and I said to Patricia: 'Do you mind if I kiss you?' or words to that effect. We stopped walking and stood on the grass verge on the left-hand side of the drive. She laid her things on the grass and I think she laid her hat there as well.

Before she did that, she was not keen on giving me a kiss, but consented in the end. I kissed her once or twice to begin with and she did not object. She then asked me to continue escorting her up the drive. I did not do so as I could not stop kissing her. As I was kissing her, I let my hand slip down her body between her coat and her clothes. Her coat was open, and my hand may have touched her breast, but I am not sure. She struggled and said, 'Don't, don't, you beast', or something like that. I struggled with her, and she said to me, 'Let me go or I will tell my father.' I then lost control of myself, and Patricia fell on the grass sobbing. She appeared to have fainted because she went limp.

I am a bit hazy about what happened next, but I probably pulled the body of Patricia through the bushes to hide it. I dragged her by her arms or hands, but I cannot remember. Even before this happened, I do not think I was capable of knowing what I was doing. I was confused at the time and I believe I stabbed her one or twice with my service knife. I had been carrying this in my trouser pocket. I am not sure what kind of knife it was. I may have caught her by the throat to stop her from shouting. I may have pushed her scarves against her mouth to stop her shouting. It is all very hazy. I think I was disturbed either by seeing a light or hearing footsteps in the drive.

I must have remained hidden and later walked out of the Glen at the gate lodge on to the main road [Shore Road]. As far as I know, I crossed the main road and threw the knife into the sea. I felt that something awful must have happened and quickly walked back to the camp. I went to my billet and arrived there at roughly 6.30pm. There was no one at the billet at the time. I saw that I had some small patches of Patricia's blood on my flannels. I took a fairly large wooden nail brush from my kit. I got some soap and water from the ablutions and scrubbed the blood off my flannels. I must have done this, but I do not quite remember. As far as I know, no person saw me doing it.

I then went to our central registry and did some typing as I was preparing for an examination. I went to bed between 9.30pm and 10pm. I got up roughly at about 7am on Thursday 13

November 1952. I had my breakfast and did my routine duties. At between 8.15 am and 8.30am that day the postman was delivering mail to our camp and he told me that Mr Justice Curran's daughter had been found dead in the grounds. He may have said she had been shot; I cannot just remember. At about 4pm that day, the RAF police came to the camp, checking on our movements for the previous evening.

Gordon went on to describe the preliminary investigation by the RAF police in which his locker, amongst others, was searched, and his clothes examined, and the subsequent investigation but added little to what he had given in previous accounts. About concocting an alibi, he offered this explanation:

> Corporal Connor from the camp and I agreed to say that we were in the camp together and had tea; that as soon as we had finished, we went to the billet together. We both told this story to the RAF police, although it was untrue.

According to Capstick, Gordon stopped at this point. Kennedy's evidence was that Gordon had gone on to say: 'That's all'. Gordon then read the statement Capstick had written out, initialled some alterations and then asked for time to think before signing the statement. Kennedy told Gordon to take all the time he needed and suggested that he go downstairs to think about it. There were two RUC men in the room to which he was sent, and they spoke to him about the case, which they should not have done because he was under caution.

When Gordon returned to the room where he had been questioned, he added the following to his statement:

> I am very sorry for having killed Patricia. I had no intention whatever of killing the girl. It was solely due to a black-out. God knows as well as

anybody else that the furthest thing in my mind was to kill the girl and I ask His forgiveness. I throw myself on to the mercy of the law and I ask you to do your best for me so that I can make a complete restart in life. I should like to say how sorry I am for all the distress I have caused the Curran family. I have felt run down for some time and the black-out may have been the result of over-studying and worry generally. I am also sorry for the distress and worry I have caused my dear father and mother. I ask my parents' forgiveness and if I am spared, I shall redeem my past life.

When the confession reading ended, the defence had its only opportunity to cross-examine Capstick. McVeigh began by asking the detective about his questioning of Gordon on 10 December, just over a month before the confession, in which Gordon had denied any knowledge of the murder.

According to the defence, Capstick had taken a statement from Gordon without a caution, and written it down in his notebook, but had not asked Gordon to sign it. Capstick maintained that he had just asked Gordon about his movements and had asked 'general questions' about the murder, so there had been no need to ask Gordon to sign a statement. Had the jury been present, this might have caused members to wonder about Capstick's way of eliciting and recording evidence, but if the judge was not impressed, he gave no sign of it.

McVeigh moved on to the day of the confession. He asked Capstick about the sequence in which he and Kennedy had obtained the information laid out in Iain Gordon's confession.

The judge intervened at this point to ask Capstick to read out his note about the morning conversation with Gordon.

Capstick read:

10.20am, 15/1/53 saw Gordon at office. Dist. Insp. Nelson left him at 10.20am and I questioned him at length re masturbation, gross indecency, sodomy. And then I go on to 2.30.

Defence counsel McVeigh: 'So, you went over the whole area of indecency apparently [referring to the nearly three-hour discussion of indecency, masturbation and sodomy in the morning], when Inspector Kennedy came up [at lunchtime] there was no question of confession?'

Capstick: 'No, not the slightest. Hadn't been talking about the murder at all, there was no question about a confession.'

McVeigh: 'He had already been broken down on one incident the day before, the Connor incident?' [Gordon's admission that his alibi about having tea with Connor was false.]

Capstick: 'Yes.'

McVeigh. 'And I put it to you that you were trying to break him down on 15 January about the rest of the matter?'

Capstick: 'The rest of what matter?'

McVeigh: 'A confession about the murder.'

Capstick: 'He was broken down on masturbation. He later admitted a gross indecency with another individual, and sodomy; and eventually admitted them and quoted them then to me.'

McVeigh: 'And you say – your phrase was: "He was broken down".'

Capstick: 'Never.'

At this point the attorney general said: 'The witness did not use those words and I call for …' Whatever Warnock was calling for got lost as he, judge, McVeigh and Capstick all spoke at the same time.

When order was restored, McDermott ruled in Capstick's favour, but McVeigh continued to insist that

Capstick had said 'broken down'. The court record was sent for, and it showed that Capstick *had* used the phrase 'broke him down'. Capstick then replied that he had used the phrase only in replying to McVeigh's use of it, continuing to assert that Gordon had not been 'broken down'.

An even more fractious exchange between the judge and the lead defence counsel followed. McVeigh asked Capstick if he had told a *Daily Sketch* reporter that the defence would seek to have the trial moved to London. Capstick denied saying this, though he admitted that he had spoken to the reporter in question.

The chief justice got irritated at McVeigh's repeated attempts to get Capstick to deny under oath what he clearly had said to the reporter. All four leading knew that perjury was being committed, but McDermott made it clear that he wanted to move on.

Before McVeigh finished with Capstick, he suggested that a deal had been done between Capstick and Kennedy on the one hand and Gordon on the other, that if a confession were made, it would not contain any sexual details because Gordon wanted these to be kept from his mother.

Capstick's answer was careful. 'It was not mentioned, indecency or any sexual matters, in any statement.'

McVeigh tried again. 'May I suggest to you that it was indicated to him [Gordon] that it mightn't have been necessary for that [sexual] material to appear in a written statement?'

Capstick's denial was guarded. 'It was not indicated by me, my lord.'

McVeigh was trying to show that the confession was obtained by means of inducements, on the lines of 'confess to murder and we won't say anything about your homosexual carry-on with Wesley Courtney [about which Gordon and Desmond had spoken just before Christmas 1952] or the prostitutes you went with in Belfast'. Capstick's reply absolved himself of such dealing but left open the possibility that another policeman had made such a deal with Gordon. Had any inducements been offered, Gordon's confession would not have been admissible. Judge McDermott saw very clearly what McVeigh was driving at, as his later questions to the policeman showed.

The attorney general stood up to seek permission for further questioning of Capstick.

'Just one question. At any time during your interview with Gordon did he ever express to you that he was fatigued or wanted to desist?', Warnock asked.

'He certainly did not: no, my lord', Capstick replied.

Judge McDermott immediately posed a quickfire series of questions to Capstick.

Q. 'Was masturbation, indecency, discussed with Gordon?'

A. 'Yes.'

Q. 'These were matters which Gordon naturally would not wish to have made public?

' A. 'Yes.'.

. Q. 'Did you raise those matters to exercise some kind of hold over him?'

A. 'No.'

Q. 'Are you absolutely clear about that? '

A . 'Yes, I was just trying to find out what sort of person he was'.

Q. 'Did you ask Gordon any questions while taking down his statement/confession?'

A: 'No, nor did Inspector Kennedy.'.

And then the final question. 'I want you to give this great care in your answer', the judge said. 'Did you at any time hold out any inducement, either by promise or by threat, or otherwise?'

'No, my lord' Capstick replied. 'I am fully aware of the inducements that must not be held out, and there was no inducement, threat or anything like that held out.'

'Direct or indirect'.

'Direct or indirect, my lord', Capstick confirmed.

'Very well', said the judge.

Despite McDermott's attempt to get the prosecution case back on an even keel, there was a general feeling in court that McVeigh had just got the better of Capstick. This does not come across in the trial transcript, but lawyers and others present said as much to the BBC team making the 1995 television documentary *More Sinned Against Than Sinning?* The judge must have thought so. His intervention at the end reads like a final effort to reinforce the main points of Capstick's evidence minus McVeigh's damaging scepticism. The pity is that jury was not present to hear this.

The next witness Inspector Albert Kennedy said he was in charge of the murder investigation. He confirmed Capstick's account of Gordon dictating the confession, rather than it being obtained by question-and-answer. He also said that if on the second day of the three-day interrogation Gordon had decided to go home to Scotland, he, as the officer-in-charge of the investigation, would have allowed him to do so. Even up to lunchtime on the day of the confession, he would have allowed him to go. He also agreed that at that time, the police did not have the statement from Mrs. Mary Jackson placing Gordon in Whiteabbey at around 5pm on the day of the murder.

For the defence, John Agnew asked Kennedy about the whereabouts of other policemen during Gordon's questioning. Kennedy agreed that at different times Detective Sergeant Hawkins, Head Constable Russell, Detective Inspector Nelson, Head Constable Deveney and Sergeant McCutcheon had access to Gordon over those three days.

Kennedy denied that when Gordon had confessed to the murder and he had asked for time to consider whether or not he would sign the statement, Capstick had replied: 'It looks like we are going to have another black-out. Go downstairs until we make up our minds what we are going to do with you.' Kennedy reiterated that the confession was a voluntary statement given in Gordon's own words, rather than a narrative constructed from questions and answers.

The next witness Head Constable Samuel Deveney gave evidence of going into the room where Gordon had been sent to consider signing the confession. Deveney was then still a sergeant and he said he had gone there looking for a fellow sergeant – McCutcheon – to talk to him about an unrelated matter. He found McCutcheon in a room with Gordon, who was walking up and down between the window and the door and was talking to himself. There followed some conversation with Gordon about the Curran murder, he said. Deveney said he had not known that Gordon would be in the room, nor that he was under caution and trying to decide if he would a sign a confession or not. If he had known that he would not have spoken to him, nor would he have advised Gordon to tell the truth to Inspector Kennedy, as he had done.

Deveney denied telling Gordon that he had seen a file which said that he hadn't a dog's chance of getting off. However, he had heard Gordon say words to the effect that he would admit to the murder if he was sure his father and mother wouldn't find out [about his homosexual behaviour]. Deveney said he had not put those words in his deposition because Gordon had not been addressing him when he had spoken.

The defence called RAF camp commandant Richard Popple who confirmed that he twice told Detective Sergeant Hawkins that if a statement were to be taken from Gordon, who was then a minor, an RAF officer should have been present, and that the prosecution had ignored this advice.

At this stage, the *voir dire* to establish if the contested evidence was to be heard by the jury was still continuing. The expectation was that the attorney general, Edmond Warnock, would conclude by citing legal authorities to support his contention that the disputed confession was admissible, despite having been taken from a minor without an adult witness present. Warnock did not do so, and for the defence, McVeigh cited various authorities, insisting that Gordon had been treated unfairly, and evidence thus obtained should not go to the jury.

Without further ado, Judge McDermott ruled that Gordon's confession was admissible as a voluntary statement. 'I see no reason to think it was taken unfairly or in a manner which, in the exercise of my discretion, would justify me in excluding it.' The judge went on to say that he rejected the idea that 'the absence of some adult person renders it [the confession] inadmissible or makes it unfair that it should now be used against him'.

The chief justice ruled out one piece of evidence, and partially ruled out another. RUC Constable Herdman had said that he heard Gordon saying that the prosecution had the wrong knife at an earlier hearing before a magistrate. The chief justice ruled that Herdman's evidence that Gordon – on seeing a knife produced in court – said 'that's not it' was admissible; after that point, Herdman's evidence was inadmissible. He also ruled out the Deveney and McCutcheon exchange with Gordon in the immediate aftermath of the confession. All the rest, including the disputed confession, could be put to the jury.

At 5.25pm the jury was summoned and told that the trial was resuming. County Inspector Kennedy read Gordon's confession to the court.

At 6.20pm the court rose.

The cat was now well and truly out of the bag

Thursday 5 March 1953

The morning newspapers had headlines that editors dream of. But the *Belfast Telegraph* had got there first. A banner headline on a special late edition of Wednesday's evening paper proclaimed, perhaps more accurately than it intended, 'Gordon's alleged confession'.

A second headline told of a guilty man's remorse: 'If I am spared, I shall redeem my past life'. On the same day the *Belfast Telegraph* naughtily included – on an inside page, and well away from the court reports – a New York interview with the film director Alfred Hitchcock headlined 'Everybody loves a murder – at least on screen'.

The trial was halfway over, and so far as the prosecution was concerned, the job was almost done. The previous evening the jury had heard Inspector Albert Kennedy reading out Gordon's confession. Kennedy was now being questioned by George Hanna for the prosecution. Kennedy said he had seen Gordon with Capstick at the temporary police barracks at Whiteabbey at lunchtime on 15 January 1953. At around 2.20pm he had left them together. About 20 minutes later, he received a message from Capstick asking him to return to the interrogation room. 'When I came in, Capstick said, "Gordon has told me that he will now tell us the truth about the murder".' Gordon then said that he had killed Patricia Curran in a black-out. Kennedy formally cautioned him. Gordon had then dictated his statement which Capstick took down.

For the defence John Agnew cross-examined. With regard to the three-day interrogation, Kennedy said that on 13 January Gordon was questioned about his personal and family background, on 14 January about his whereabouts on the day of the murder, and on the morning of 15 January about sexual matters. Agnew was trying to find out if

Kennedy really was in charge of the case, or if he had given Capstick his head. Kennedy was adamant that he was in charge.

'Were you satisfied, say on the evening of 13 January, with the answers Gordon had given?'

'So far as they went, I was, yes.'

'Why was he called back on 14 January?'

'I directed that he be called back on 14 January, having read the statement of 13 January.'

Agnew went on to question Kennedy's account of the drag marks on the ground where the body had been found. He was the officer in charge of the investigation. He had seen the drag marks, so why then did a police spokesman say at a press conference two days later, 15 November, that no drag marks had been found?

Kennedy replied that he had not been at the police press conference on 15 November when the existence of drag marks had been denied. He could not account for that statement, nor had he seen it reported in the press.

Agnew then turned to a more serious matter: the serial questioning of Gordon on three consecutive days in January 1953. Kennedy argued that Gordon had been questioned for four hours on 13 January, and about the same length of time the following day. Agnew's purpose was to establish if the pattern of the questioning, beginning with Gordon's personal life on the first day, and his whereabouts at the time of the murder on the second, had the prior approval of Kennedy. Kennedy said that was so.

Agnew: 'Do you agree that over the three days that he [Gordon] was seen by a number of different police officers?'

Kennedy: 'Yes.'

Agnew: 'At any time, when he was being examined on the 13th and 14th [January] did you not come into the room shortly and go out again?'

Kennedy: 'No.'

In reply to Agnew, Kennedy agreed that District Inspector Nelson had had access to Gordon, as did Head Constable Russell on the first two days, and Head Constable Deveney and Sergeant McCutcheon for a few minutes on the third day. And that Detective Sergeant Hawkins had access to Gordon during the second and third days.

Kennedy denied that he was responsible for a press report on 14 January 1953 – the day before the confession – which said that Capstick and Hawkins were returning to London at the weekend, and that their job was done.

Agnew then came to a major element of the confession: whether it truly was a voluntary statement that Gordon had dictated, as the police maintained, or a series of answers to questions written down by Capstick to read as if it were a single narrative?

Agnew: 'I put it to you that during the course of that statement [the confession], the accused was asked a large number of questions?'

Kennedy: 'He was not, my lord.'

Agnew gave an example of what he took to be Gordon's answers with Capstick's questions edited out: 'I was in there for about five to ten minutes and then went to Quiery's newspaper shop. I would not be in there very long.' Kennedy denied that this was the answer to a question.

Agnew continued to press him, offering another passage which suggested a question-and-answer, 'I believe I called in at the bookies, approximately opposite Quiery's but off the main road. I placed a bet there on a horse for one of the airmen at the camp. I forget his name.'

Agnew asked if Gordon really added 'I forget his name' without one of the policemen asking who it was.

'Mr Capstick wrote down what was said', Kennedy replied.

In all Agnew quoted more than 40 instances of what he maintained were questions put to Gordon but transcribed in the confession as if they had been voluntary statements. Kennedy denied each one.

In reply to a question about how the confession had been transcribed, Kennedy replied: 'Just sentence by sentence. At times the sentences were longer than others because he [Gordon] spoke rather quickly and I asked him to take his time and watch Mr Capstick's hand so that he could get [take] down what Mr Capstick was saying.'

Agnew: 'What was his condition – tired or confused or alert?'

Kennedy: 'I would describe him as being alert, concentrating on what he was saying, and being careful about what he was saying. He displayed no sign of tiredness or fatigue, as far as I could see, and he certainly made no complaint of being that way.'

Judge McDermott was clearly unhappy with the defence line of questioning, as several interventions showed. Agnew was not fazed, he listened to what the judge had said, changed tack slightly and kept going, but in the end, he failed to shift Kennedy on the question of voluntary confession versus interrogation masked as a confession. After the cross-examination had ended, the judge took the unusual step of offering the jury the option of asking Inspector Kennedy questions, but none did, so he left the witness box.

The court record does not state this, except obliquely, but something very odd had just happened. Inspector Albert Kennedy had given Superintendent John Capstick's evidence for him. Missing was evidence from John Capstick, the policeman who had obtained the confession. Instead, Albert Kennedy, who admitted he only played a supporting role, took the stand to answer for the confession. The defence had not been allowed to cross-examine in front of the jury the most important prosecution witness – the London policeman who had 'broken' Gordon. The jury did not get to assess the credibility of Capstick's evidence as it came from his own mouth. There is an echo here of Capstick's Ghost Squad tactic of breaking open an investigation but leaving the nitty-gritty of collecting and presenting evidence to others.

Constable Edward Rutherford was next. He had been roused from his bed in the early hours of Thursday, 13 November, and was told to go to Glen House, he said. He got there about 2am and met the judge in the avenue. Together they went along the avenue and saw a light in the undergrowth. They made for it and found the body of Patricia Curran, lying under a tree. Standing beside her, holding a torch, was her brother Desmond.

'The body was on its back, the head was towards the river on the left, and with the feet towards the avenue. The body was straight with the head slightly towards the left', Rutherford told Bradley McCall, the most junior member of the prosecution's legal team. A minute or two later, the solicitor Malcolm Davison arrived on the scene. There were now four men gathered around the body lying in the undergrowth, Lance Curran, his son Desmond, Davison and Constable Russell. It appears that Doreen Davison, who had driven her husband to the scene, remained in the car.

'The judge, Mr. Davison and Desmond Curran carried the body to Mrs. Davison's car', Rutherford said. He, having taken measurements at the scene, went back to the police barracks, leaving the lighted torch to mark the spot where the body was found. Later he and Sergeant William Black and a detective constable [name redacted] went to the place where the body had been found, and District Inspector Mahaffy joined them. He, Rutherford, had observed some articles lying in the general area where the body had lain 'what appeared to be a bag, a handbag and a piece of yellow cloth'. In cross-examination, McVeigh failed to ask Rutherford why he had not seen these articles before.

The Curran family's solicitor, Malcolm Davison, was next into the witness box. His wife had answered a phone call from the judge at about 1.40am on the morning of Thursday, 13 November. Shortly afterwards they had driven up the avenue approaching Glen House. About 20 or 30 yards into the undergrowth on the left-hand side of the avenue, they saw Desmond Curran holding a torch and standing over the body of his sister. Rutherford and the judge had just arrived. Desmond Curran, his father and Malcolm Davison carried the body to the car to take it to Dr. Wilson's house nearby. In Malcolm Davison's account, Constable Rutherford helped to carry the body, but the policeman had not said that. The legs had become rigid, and they had difficulty getting the body into the car.

Dr. Kenneth Wilson gave evidence that he was the Curran family's doctor. He was roused from his bed at 2.20am on 13 November. When he went to his front door, he found the judge and Malcolm and Doreen Davison there, and they carried the body of Patricia Curran into his surgery. He examined her and found she was dead. He told her father this sad news. Initially he thought she might have been shot by a shotgun, and that she could have been dead for four hours. A pathologist, Dr. Albert Wells, was summoned. He arrived around 5am, and the body was removed to the mortuary in Belfast. Strangely, Dr Wilson makes no mention of Desmond Curran being among the people who brought Patricia Curran's body to his house. Many years later he confirmed that not only had Lance been present then, but so also was his son Desmond. More than one car would have been needed to transport the two Davisons, Desmond and Lance Curran and the body to Dr. Wilson's house.

AN RUC constable Thomas McAnallen was called. He was stationed at Whiteabbey, he said. He had been ordered to stand guard over the body of a young woman at Dr. Wilson's surgery in Whiteabbey from 9.05am on 13 November 13. He accompanied the body to Belfast City Morgue at around 3pm, where Detective-Sergeant Samuel Deveney took custody of it.

Deveney, then attached to Lisburn police station, gave evidence about being sent to Dr. Wilson's house at about 4.30am on 13 November and seeing Patricia Curran's body there. He later went to the place where it had been found. He gave details of an experiment that he had conducted on Patricia Curran's portfolio which had been found neatly placed, according to the prosecution, eleven inches from the grass verge of the avenue. The body was about 40 feet further into the undergrowth under a tree. The portfolio was essentially a stiff folder containing textbooks, notepads and a letter. Deveney later showed that Patricia Curran could not have dropped the portfolio in the course of a struggle. He had dropped the portfolio and its contents from varying heights, and each time the contents had spilled out.

As he admitted in cross-examination, the experiment had been carried out indoors on a floor covered by two mats. The defence contended that to be conclusive the test should have been carried out on similar terrain to where the body was found. At this remove, it is hard to see what point the defence was making. Admittedly the experiment was performed fairly crudely, but it is hard to see what difference an outdoor re-enactment would have made.

The defence missed a significant point. If the portfolio had been in the open at the side of the avenue, not under a tree as the body had been since around five-thirty or six pm the previous evening according to the prosecution, it should have been wet from rainfall. The defence missed an opportunity to suggest that the portfolio had been placed in the avenue *after* the body was found. It should also have been seen by those who came and went from Glen House after Patricia made her way up the avenue.

Deveney also said he had seen a 40-yard track mark where the body was found. 'The mark was consistent with someone having been dragged from the point where the shoes were found to near the tree where the body was found.'

He had also seen a leaf with blood drops on it twelve inches away from where [Patricia Curran's] shoes had been found near the avenue, and a similar leaf three feet away in the direction of where the body was found. Seven feet farther on, in the same direction, he had found a button which was similar to those missing on the victim's coat. Another blood-spattered leaf had been found close to the tree where the body was found.

Under cross-examination, Deveney defended his experiment with the falling portfolio. He also said that he had not known that Gordon had been making a statement under caution when he witnessed him walking up and down and talking to himself at the temporary police station on 15 January during Gordon's break in his confession to the murder. Deveney insisted that he would not have spoken to Gordon about the case had he been aware of that. The judge immediately intervened.

Judge McDermott: 'You didn't know then that he [Gordon] had been making a statement under caution?'

Deveney: 'I did not, my lord.'

McDermott: 'You do know it now?'

Deveney: 'I do.'

Mrs Hetty Lyttle of Harmony Place, Whiteabbey, took the stand. She had left her job at the weaving factory at six pm on Wednesday, 12 November. With her friend Mrs Currie, she went to a newsagent to change her books at the revolving library. In pre-TV days , many newsagents kept a shelf of books, usually romances and detective stories, for lending to customers for a few pence a week. On their way back from the newsagent, she and Mrs Currie stopped outside the gate of the Glen. By the light of the streetlamp, she saw a man leaving the avenue. After hesitating for a moment, he passed the two women.

'He had [on] a dustcoat and he looked pale', she said.

'What direction was he going?' George Hanna, for the prosecution, asked her.

'Towards the tide', Mrs Lyttle responded. By that she meant Belfast Lough. 'Down the tide', or 'down the water' was what local people said when they were talking about the shore of the lough.

This was about 6.10pm. More than two months later, on 23 January 1953, after Gordon had been charged and his photograph had been published widely, Mrs Lyttle had picked out Gordon at an identity parade as the man she had seen.

McVeigh cross-examined for the defence. Mrs Lyttle agreed that there had been a car parked on the road nearby at the time she saw the pale man leaving the avenue to Glen House. McVeigh was trying to make the point that there were other men in the vicinity at the time. Mrs Lyttle said she had first given a statement to the police eight days after the murder. She agreed that she was a regular reader of the *Belfast Telegraph*. On the evening of 16 January, the day after Gordon's arrest, the *Telegraph* published a photograph of him on the front page, but Mrs Lyttle hadn't seen it, she said, because she was preparing dinner for her husband and family.

McVeigh: 'I suppose the family were talking about it [the photograph of Gordon]?'

Lyttle: 'Yes.'

McVeigh: 'And were you interested enough to look at the photo?'

Lyttle: 'I hadn't time to look at the photo.'

The judge intervened. 'Did you look at the photo counsel is talking about?'

Lyttle: 'No, your lordship, I didn't.'

Sometime later, when Mrs Lyttle's testimony was about to conclude, the judge spoke to her again and told her to look at the man in the dock. 'Can you say whether he was the man who came out on the evening of 12 November from the Glen as you were passing, or do you only think he was like the man? Tell me exactly what you feel about that?'

Lyttle: 'Well, I think he was the man.'

Judge: 'Very well, thank you.'

Two points arise about Mrs Lyttle's testimony. She identified Gordon after he had been charged, and after the announcement of a reward, and also, she said nothing about his black eye which others had noticed. Neither prosecution nor defence called Mrs Lyttle's companion, Mrs Agnes Currie. She had told the police that she had been with Mrs Lyttle on that day but had no recollection of seeing a man leaving the avenue. The court rose for lunch after hearing evidence about the conduct of the identity parade.

The hearing resumed at 2.30pm with evidence from Aircraftman William Scott, who said that Gordon had asked him and others for an alibi for the afternoon of the murder. This was when the RAF police were questioning conscripts about their movements. He also testified that within the barracks Gordon kept to himself and had no particular friend or friends there.

Another conscript, Leading Aircraftman John Cuthbert, gave evidence of Gordon having said to him and others. 'You'd think that you blokes would stand up and say you saw me'.

Douglas Walsh, an RAF teleprinter operator, said he was working at Edenmore in November 1952. He saw Gordon in a pub, the Ulster Saloon in Whiteabbey, some weeks after the murder. When the bar closed, they walked back together to Edenmore. On the way, Gordon asked Walsh if he had seen him on the night of 12 November and Scott said he hadn't. Gordon had then gone on to say: 'If I had a friend, a very good friend, and he was in trouble, even serious trouble, I would be prepared to lie for him, or words to that effect', Walsh said. 'I told him that such a mentality was very funny, and it was all wrong.' Walsh also said that Gordon kept apart from the other men in the camp. He was 'an odd sort of fellow', he said.

NAAFI attendant Sadie Smyth gave evidence of lending a scrubbing brush to Gordon about three or four weeks after the murder. She recalled that he looked pale and worried at the time. On the morning after the murder, she said she recalled Gordon saying to her: 'I wish you had been in the NAAFI yesterday instead of Irene, because Irene can't remember what time I came into the NAAFI last night.'

After cross-examination, the judge said: 'It doesn't seem to me that the scrubbing brush comes into it; it was quite a usual thing in the RAF to get a scrubbing brush from the NAAFI before you look your best.'

The next witness, Dr. Albert Wells, registrar in pathology at Royal Victoria Hospital Belfast, had rather more to contribute. He had been called to the house of Dr. Wilson at Whiteabbey at 5am on Thursday, 13 November 1952, and examined the body of Patricia Curran. The body was almost fully clothed, he said. There were heavy blood stains on the left-hand side of her jumper, but it was not so marked on the right. 'There were five tears about a quarter of an inch long running down the right side in the front of the skirt; the knickers were torn on the right side and they were stained with blood. The stockings were properly in place. The knees and the heel were stained with soil, and there was a wound on the right side of the thigh.' Wells deduced that the victim had been standing when that wound was inflicted, 'but that later blood had flowed from her thighs downwards; she had changed position and was then likely to have been lying on her back'. Her body temperature and the state of rigor mortis he had found indicated that she had died in the twelve hours before he examined her.

Later that day Dr. Wells had performed a post-mortem examination at the mortuary. Patricia Curran was five feet eight inches tall, weighed nine stone and was well-nourished.

Dr. Wells said: 'I formed the opinion that death was due to, firstly shock called by haemorrhage from multiple stab wounds, inflicted on the chest, scalp, abdomen and right thigh, some of which had penetrated to involve both lungs, heart and liver. And secondly heart failure, due to haemorrhage into the heart, pericardial (sic).'He appears to be saying that puncturing the pericardial sac, which surrounds the heart, allowed fluid to flow into the heart, causing it to fail.

Patricia Curran had been stabbed 37 times. She had suffered twelve major wounds, eleven on the chest, and one on the thigh. Any one of eight such wounds could have killed her.

Dr. Wells was shown a knife: exhibit X19. He agreed that a knife like that could have been responsible for some wounds, but not all. A wound on the chin could have been caused by a direct blow, another to the corner of the lip was 'caused by direct violence, with a blunt instrument'. Asked what kind of instrument, Dr. Wells said that many kinds were possible, but he suggested 'a fist or a boot or any heavy object'.

Under cross-examination by the defence, Dr Wells said that pattern of cuts in the victim's skirt did not match the pattern of stab wounds to the body. 'As far as I was concerned, they could have been caused by catching the skirt on barbed wire.'

He agreed that the stab wounds were widespread and indiscriminate, and 'some at least required a very great degree of violence'. The blow that fractured the sixth rib on the left was an example of what he meant, he said.

The pathologist said that he didn't think it likely that the blows and stab wounds had been inflicted by one person maintaining a fixed position. As the attack developed, the victim could have been dying on her feet. She might have been able to walk a bit after the attack had begun, but as the blows continued, she was likely to have fallen to the ground and her heart would have given out. He also said that he had found about a pint of blood in each of the victim's pleural cavities, and about four fluid ounces in the pericardial sac.

Two pages of Dr. Wells's testimony remain redacted from the court record held at the Public Record Office of Northern Ireland. Campaigners for Gordon, who saw an unredacted version of this testimony, maintain the missing material raises questions about the role of RUC detective Samuel Deveney. He took custody of Patricia Curran's body at Dr. Wilson's house and had it taken to the morgue. There, they said, he undressed her body prior to the post-mortem examination. Also redacted is Dr Well's finding that Patricia Curran was a virgin when she died. This redaction may have contributed to the impression that her 'promiscuous' behaviour was a factor in her death.

RUC Constable Charlton Herdman was called next. Exhibit X19, the knife which had been produced when Dr. Wells was in the witness box, now made another appearance in evidence which the defence had sought to have excluded. Herdman said he had escorted Gordon to a court hearing on 5 February 1953, at which depositions were taken. Herdman said he was sitting beside the prisoner Gordon in court. Kennedy held the knife in his hand as he gave evidence. Gordon was watching the policeman intently, Herdman said, Kennedy accidentally let the knife slip to the floor. Gordon then turned to Herdman and said: 'That's not it'. This intervention would count against Gordon – did he mean that there was another knife, the 'right' one, which was used to murder Patricia? And how could he know this – unless he was the murderer?

After the jury had returned from their afternoon tea break, Denis Hawkins took the witness stand. He said that he was a detective sergeant from Scotland Yard, and he gave evidence of examining clothes taken from Gordon on 29 November 1952 on which he could find no traces of blood. He had handed these articles, along with others received from the RUC, to Dr. Firth for examination. (Firth was about to be called to give evidence and his role became clear then)] They amounted to 64 items, including eight neckties, underwear, towels and other personal possessions, and were listed in exhibit K23 in the trial proceedings, he told George Hanna for the prosecution.

Questions shifted to 13 January, the first of three days of Gordon's interrogation. Hawkins and Head Constable Russell had interviewed Gordon in the morning and afternoon at the RUC barracks at Edenmore. In cross-examination by Basil Kelly for the defence, Hawkins agreed that the camp commandant, Richard Popple, had twice told him that an RAF officer should be present when Gordon was questioned, but that he chosen to ignore that request. Neither he nor Kennedy had cautioned Gordon before the questioning began.

Kelly: 'And all day on 13 January was he questioned about his private life? About matters pertaining to his sexual life?'

Hawkins: 'In some respects, yes.'

Hawkins went to say that sexual matters were within the scope of his inquiry. He agreed that on the previous day his superior officer Capstick had said that sexual matters were not within the scope of his inquiry. The two men differed on that point; Hawkins admitted.

'Am I right in describing your questioning on 13 January as a "pressing examination"?'

'Pressing, sir, but not overbearing by any means. The questioning was persistent', Hawkins replied. Gordon would later maintain that Russell shouted at him repeatedly.

On the first day, 13 January, Gordon had been questioned from 10am to 12.15pm, and then from 3pm to 4pm, Hawkins said. The following day, the interrogation had begun at 10am and continued until 1.30pm, and from 3pm to 4pm. In fact, Gordon began to be questioned around 9.45am, according to Capstick, who started interrogating Gordon before Hawkins arrived, and then withdrew. The afternoon session had lasted beyond 4.30pm, Hawkins admitted.

Following cross-examination, the prosecution sought to have the statement Hawkins wrote as a result of the two days of questioning admitted as evidence. For the defence, John Agnew opposed the introduction of that statement. He argued that it was improper to bring it in after Hawkins had given his evidence and had been cross-examined. The judge pointed out that Basil Kelly for the defence had argued that the questioning of Gordon had been oppressive. Kelly, in raising the question of how the statement was compiled had brought it 'into play'. The judge ruled that the prosecution was 'entitled to produce the statement for the purpose of relying on it as indicating, if they can, the nature of the inquiry which produced it'. It was a fine legal point, and as so often happened in this trial, the judge ruled against Gordon's legal team.

Hawkins then read the statement in open court.

When he reached a passage: 'At this time [October 1952] I was friendly with a nurse. We were walking out together, we never courted. She is a nurse at the Royal Victoria Hospital ...', the attorney general interrupted and told the policeman to omit the woman's name. Later Hawkins was told by the judge not to name Wesley Courtney, the barber with whom Gordon had sex.

The statement amounted to almost 3,000 words and must have taken 20 to 25 minutes to read aloud. In it, Gordon first repeated but later withdrew the alibi that he had relied on since he was first asked about his movements between 5pm and 6.00pm on the day of the murder. Instead, he said that when he had been having his tea in the NAAFI, an RAF policeman stuck his head in the door and shouted to all the men present: 'Arrange between yourselves who you were with between five and six pm last night'. Connor approached Gordon and said: 'You may say you were sitting with me.'

Connor had given no reason for saying this, Gordon said. At first, he had refused Connor's offer, saying that it wasn't true – he wasn't with Connor, but another airman said it didn't matter. Connor told him not to worry – it would be all right. Gordon went along with it, even though it wasn't true. In fact, he'd had tea alone in the dining room and shortly after 5pm went back to the central registry where he practised his typing for an upcoming examination. He had remained there alone until after 7pm. Gordon's statement concluded by saying that he never carried a screwdriver or penknife in his pocket, nor had he been in the avenue leading to Glen House on the Wednesday evening.

In the further cross-examination which followed the reading of the statement, Hawkins told Basil Kelly for the defence that he had no doubt that Gordon had changed his story about his alibi 'as a result of my persistent questioning'. Gordon had gone silent for two minutes in between saying: 'I want to tell you the truth' and changing his story about the alibi.

Kelly wanted to know why Hawkins did not caution Gordon then, because he must have known that Gordon was about to incriminate himself. Hawkins replied that he never cautioned a man 'until I have good reason to arrest him, and I had no reason to arrest him.'

Hawkins agreed with Kelly that the statement reflected the answers to questions put by Russell and himself to Gordon over two days, and he had written them down, and Gordon had signed every page of the document.

The final witness of the day was Dr James Firth of the British Home Office forensic science laboratory at Preston, Lancashire, which provided expert services to the RUC in cases such as this one. He had examined Patricia Curran's body at the hospital mortuary on 14 November, the day after the body was found. His evidence mainly concerned the state of her body and her clothing. The prosecution had attempted to connect with the murder the residue of a bloodstain found on Gordon's trousers. The discussion was complex but, in the end, McVeigh was able to show that the bloodstain, of which very little remained, had predated the murder. Dr Firth also noted that Gordon had the same O blood group as Patricia Curran. McVeigh got Dr. Firth to confirm that that there no scratches on her body when he examined it, but there were scratches on her face. Her knickers were torn but had remained in place. No seminal fluid was found. Exchanges between McDermott and McVeigh were noticeably tetchy by this stage, though no major point of dispute arose. It was a few minutes past six pm, and the judge adjourned until the following day

Friday 6 March 1953

The first witness on the second last day of the trial was Desmond Curran. He was also the final witness for the prosecution. Questioned by attorney general Edmond Warnock, Desmond Curran said he had returned home at around 9pm on 12 November 1952 and gone to bed at around 11pm. His mother had woken him at about 1.30am and had driven him to a house on the main road. They stopped at one house to 'make certain inquiries' he said, meaning that they asked if anyone had seen his sister. They had borrowed a torch at a second house they called to, and he set about searching for his sister who had not come home. At that stage his father had already contacted the police, he said.

Desmond Curran searched the shrubbery along the avenue and found his sister lying grievously injured in the undergrowth. He thought she was still breathing. Very shortly afterwards his father and a policeman came along. They were soon joined by Malcolm Davison and his wife. They, thinking Patricia was still alive, lifted her into Davison's car and took her to Dr. Wilson's house.

Desmond Curran said he knew the accused, Iain Hay Gordon. He had first met him at church in Whiteabbey some months earlier and had invited him home for lunch. [Elsewhere Curran said he had met Gordon in late 1951, a year earlier.] Gordon had visited the Curran family home three times and had twice met his sister Patricia. Often when Desmond Curran went to church on Sunday, his sister accompanied him, but he could not say if she had spoken to or acknowledged Iain Hay Gordon there.

On 23 December 1953 Gordon had telephoned Curran and asked to meet him. They had gone to a café in Wellington Place, Belfast. Gordon had offered his sympathy on Patricia's death, and a long conversation about the murder ensued. The attorney general said he did not want details of that conversation, but he asked Desmond Curran what they did afterwards. Curran said they walked up the Malone Road to the Presbyterian Hostel in Howard Street, where Gordon had stayed in the past, and took the lift to an upstairs room.

Warnock: 'As the lift was ascending did Gordon make any remark to you?'

Curran: 'He said: "Now we go up to the heavens" and he then turned rather pale, and it seemed ' At this point the judge intervened and the attorney general told Curran that the judge was taking notes and he should watch his pen and allow him to catch up.

Curran continued: 'And it seemed to me that he [Gordon] said: "Someone will be asleep in about five minutes".' Curran went on to say that Gordon became very pale for a few moments.

When the two men got to a public room in the hostel, there were others present, so they decided to continue their conversation while walking. They parted at Smithfield bus station, where Gordon took the 11pm bus to Whiteabbey.

Cross-examined by John Agnew for the defence, Desmond Curran admitted that he had initiated the conversation about the murder with Gordon.

Agnew: 'And is it a fact that he said it was a painful a subject for you and he would only discuss it if you were willing, or words to that effect?'

Curran: 'He may have said that, my lord, but I cannot recollect him saying it'. When the cross-examination ended, the attorney general said that that concluded the prosecution case.

Head Constable Deveney was then recalled briefly to clarify a piece of evidence about the victim's underwear. He said that Miss Curran's brassiere straps had been intact when the body was discovered, and they had been cut when removing them for the autopsy. In doing so, he indirectly confirmed the defence belief that he was omnipresent throughout the police investigation.

The case for the defence then began. After the customary remarks about the prosecution having to prove Gordon guilty rather than the accused striving to prove his innocence, Bertie McVeigh began with the circumstances in which the confession was obtained. He described three days of close questioning of a young man who was legally a minor. 'It is for you decide', he told the jury, 'whether he was really in virtual custody.'

There was no relative there; no officers from the air force, McVeigh told the jury. They could easily have had one – they were just beside Edenmore. Why didn't they have Pilot Officer Popple down, or some responsible officer? Why didn't they send over to Scotland for Gordon's father? Why did they persist with the questioning, day after day, when they knew the views of the Royal Air Force? 'And why, on 15 January, on that morning, was he [Gordon] left alone with Superintendent Capstick for three hours? Three hours alone with him, talking apparently about sexual matters. Do you think he [Gordon] wanted to talk about sexual matters? What kind of conversation did they have? Why was he left alone with this man from Scotland Yard, [with] no member of the Royal Ulster Constabulary present, not a relative present, nor an officer of the Royal Air Force present? Why do you think he was left alone with Superintendent Capstick? Why isn't Superintendent Capstick put into the box to tell us what happened in those three hours? Is he afraid to go into the witness box and subject himself to cross-examination? Why doesn't he go in there today and tell you about what happened in those three hours, this man from Scotland Yard? A man who as superintendent has wide experience of dealing with criminals, a man who knows all the rogues, and he is left alone for three hours with this man. He [Gordon] wasn't a man, he wasn't of legal age, left alone with him [Capstick] for three hours?'

McVeigh went on to suggest that the reason the lunch break was delayed on the third consecutive day of questioning, 15 January, was to put pressure on Gordon to say what the police wanted. Would members of the jury think this was right if that had happened to their sons?

Then McVeigh turned his attention to the break during the afternoon of the confession in which Gordon was observed by RUC witnesses to be talking to himself. 'Do you think that a person who had been reduced to that state of talking and mumbling to himself hadn't been subjected to some ordeal in that room?

Not one shred of evidence had been found linking Gordon to the murder. No buttons, no footprints, nothing at all found where the body was lying. Nothing on the victim, no hairs, nothing from his coat, the forensic laboratory had found nothing at all. What of the minute blood stain? Dr. Firth had said it may have come from a cut finger, anybody's cut finger. A blood stain on a patch on Gordon's trousers turned out to predate the murder, so there was no support for the prosecution case there. McVeigh dismissed evidence about a tear in the victim's knickers as fatuous speculation. He was equally dismissive of the knife the crown produced subsequent to the disputed confession.

Mrs. Lyttle's identification of Iain Gordon at the identity parade was hesitant and unconvincing he said, and he simply did not believe her when she said she hadn't looked at the newspaper photograph of Iain Gordon before the identity parade. 'The murder was a matter of tremendous interest all over Northern Ireland, and most of all in Whiteabbey, and she says she never had the interest or the curiosity to look at the photograph of the accused. Wouldn't your immediate reaction be to say: "Let me see, let me see what he looks like"?'

Why hadn't her companion Mrs. Currie been called as a witness?

McVeigh suggested that when the police came around investigating reported crime, it was common practice for the men in the barracks to give one another alibis, whether true or not. It suited the RAF police and everyone else in the barracks if all the servicemen had alibis for whatever the civilian police force was investigating.

He asked the jury not to see the confession as backing up the rest of the evidence, unsatisfactory though it was. The test for the confession was to ask themselves: 'Is that the sort of document that a jury of twelve stout-hearted men, independent men, should act upon?'

The prosecution needed to prove criminal intent, and it had failed to do so. The defence would call witnesses to show that the accused was not responsible for his actions and could not be responsible for the alleged crime. 'Was the accused labouring under such a defect of reason from a disease of the mind as not to know the nature and quality of the act he was doing?'

At this point, McVeigh had taken a bold step. He had conceded that Gordon could have carried out the murder while he was not in his right mind. In doing this the defence effectively discarded much of the value of its earlier objections to the confession, and the total lack of any forensic evidence linking Gordon to the victim. A lawyer would understand what McVeigh was doing, but was it prudent to expect members of the jury to do so? It was a bold throw of the dice and, fortunately for McVeigh and his client, the jury chose to go along with it. But Gordon would pay for this stratagem for the rest of his life. McVeigh had no alternative because of the danger that Gordon would hang.

McVeigh told the jury that he was going to show them that under the 'McNaughten Rules' on insanity in criminal offences that Gordon was not culpable because at the time he killed Patricia Curran he was not aware of what he was doing. (The McNaughten Rules have since been replaced by more up-to-date guidance on what constitutes insanity in court cases.)

But first he went into Gordon's background. In summary, he described a vulnerable youth, one who didn't fit in well, anxious to please but reluctant to accept criticism. As a young man, he was a regular churchgoer. McVeigh said:

'You will hear how he was a very willing boy, tried to do his best, but never could do a thing really properly, and a peculiar restlessness came out. He was getting up before all the other fellows to be spick-and-span on parade, and then he would turn up with egg on his face and soap not washed off his face, and so on.'

Gordon's defence counsel went on to anticipate defence evidence, not yet given, of an incident when his client was being told by a senior officer to 'run over to the registry', whereupon Gordon had left at speed, not waiting to be told what he needed to do there. McVeigh told the jury, 'You may not think these things are of the highest importance, but they are all pointers; they show the kind of person you are dealing with.'

The first witness for the defence was Iain Gordon's mother, Brenda. She said she was a teacher married to a mining engineer, and that her son Iain had been born in 1932 in Rangoon, then the capital of Burma. She and her husband Douglas lived at Tharawaddy, about 75 miles from Rangoon. Iain had been the only European child in that area.

Asked about his temperament, Brenda Gordon said her son was 'always highly strung, always rather difficult to understand, and very, very sensitive'.

The family returned home to Scotland on leave in 1938, and Iain attended Dollar Academy in Clackmannanshire, as a day pupil. He suffered an ear infection and was sent to hospital in Edinburgh for treatment. He returned to Dollar Academy and stayed there as a boarder when his parents returned to Burma. He was then just seven years old.

In 1940, after World War II had begun, Brenda Gordon said she had flown back to Scotland and taken Iain out of school, and they travelled back to Burma, sailing from Liverpool as part of a large convoy. The journey took about three months. Iain then attended a mission school in the hills because there was no school in Tharawaddy. At the mission school his fellow pupils were Americans, Indians and Burmese. Soon after they arrived back in Burma, Iain became seriously ill and was operated on for appendicitis.

In 1942, Japan invaded Burma, and Brenda Gordon, Iain and his two-year-old baby brother, Richard, were evacuated to Bombay. They spent three days at an airfield waiting for a plane to take them out. Her husband remained on with others 'to demolish the oilfield', as she said, to keep it out of enemy hands. In India, they were sent to a refugee camp near Bombay. Conditions there were very bad, she said, and all Iain's hair fell out. A doctor said that Iain's hair loss had been caused by nervous tension.

She decided they had to leave the camp, so she and her sons moved to Poona, a hill station.

Basil Kelly: 'Were you in good health?'

Brenda Gordon: 'No, I had malaria. All the time.'

Basil Kelly: 'Were you in a number of hospitals?'

Brenda Gordon: 'The only hospital I was in was in Poona, for three weeks, but I was under treatment for much longer.'

Basil Kelly: 'During the time that you were in hospital, who was looking after Iain?'

Brenda Gordon: 'Nobody.'

The judge: 'What?'

Brenda Gordon: 'Nobody.'

This was in 1943, so Iain was about eleven years old, she told defence counsel. Iain attended a school five miles from where they were living. One day he missed his bus stop on his return journey. He was found wandering about with no idea where he was, or how to explain where he wanted to go. He had been out in the sun for more than two hours and was suffering from sunstroke.

By this stage Iain also had malaria, and it was decided in May 1943 that she and her sons go home. They endured a horrendous voyage, never being allowed to leave the ship, or to write or receive letters. Alarms warning of imminent attack by submarine or from the air rang daily. Brenda Gordon described the voyage to Basil Kelly:

'The crew had had a very bad voyage out, it had lasted – I forget how many months – an exceptionally long voyage – and the crew were suffering from strain, I think. Most of the passengers were shipwrecked crewmen who were being taken home to be placed on other boats. They too were suffering from strain; some were very ill. They mostly spent the time drinking. When the alarms went off, several passengers became hysterical.'

She had tried to shield Iain, but it was impossible. They had been stuck at Gibraltar for ten days, with depth charges going off around the ship, while they waited anxiously to join a convoy for the last leg of the journey to Liverpool. Her husband eventually made it home from Asia in 1945.

Back in Scotland, Iain returned to Dollar Academy until 1949, but he didn't make friends there. He wasn't an outstanding student. At Dollar, which was regarded as a good school, Gordon's main claim to fame was as a runner; the mile and half-mile were his best events. At home, in his teenage years, the boy became difficult for his parents to handle.

Kelly: 'Do you recall any incident when you corrected him when he was about seventeen?'

Brenda Gordon: 'Yes. I had occasion to correct him. He flew into what I thought was a violent temper and pushed his fist through a window.'

Kelly: 'And after this incident – immediately afterwards – did you notice anything peculiar about him?'

Brenda Gordon: 'Immediately afterwards he was very white and very quiet, very, very quiet.'

Kelly: 'Around this time did he develop an interest in religion?'

Brenda Gordon: 'He had always spent the greater part of his time reading books of every kind, and he seemed to become very interested in religion. And at this time, he was asked to read the lessons in the church at Dollar, which he did.'

Mrs. Gordon said that she had spoken to her sister, a doctor who was studying psychiatry, about her worries regarding Iain. Dr. Hilda Webber had given her some advice, but she had not followed it because Iain was about to begin his national service and would be examined medically then. Mrs. Gordon did not say what her sister's advice was, but she admitted that she had later regretted not acting upon it.

After joining the RAF, Iain wrote to his mother to say that he was going to dancing classes in Belfast. 'That was the first time he had shown any sign of wanting to mix with other people'.

Kelly: 'Did you ever see any sign of anything peculiar at the time?'

Brenda Gordon: 'Well I could only judge by his letters, by the writing. I always knew when he was emotionally excited because the writing became large and very irregular.'

Kelly: 'What about his school record?'

Brenda Gordon: 'It is very difficult to say, because he was so erratic. He might do a very good piece of work, then follow it by an exceedingly bad piece … as far as his record went, he didn't do very much.'

The judge asked what subjects he was good at.

'English and history', Mrs Gordon replied.

Edmond Warnock began to cross-examine Brenda Gordon. 'I think he went up for the matriculation [entrance] examination of London University? You were a school-teacher, and you knew that was a moderately stiff test?'

Brenda Gordon: 'Yes, my lord.'

Warnock: 'It was a pretty good performance for a boy of his educational background. His education had been interrupted and he was only eighteen years of age and he had spent considerable time in India?'

Mrs. Gordon agreed.

Warnock continued: 'I put it to you that there must be thousands and thousands and thousands of people living in England today whose parents were in Rangoon, India and other places and spent the earlier part of their lives in hot countries, and it doesn't produce any abnormal effect on their afterlife?'

How Warnock could have asked that, having just heard Brenda Gordon's account of the hardships, serious illnesses, interruptions to his education and other misfortunes that befell her son Iain in childhood, defies comprehension.

Mrs. Gordon replied: 'That is so, but of all the children I knew in Burma, he was the only one who did not have the advantage of the company of other children .'To the judge, she said she never saw her son Iain doing anything cruel.

The court was adjourned for lunch, and when it resumed Brenda Gordon's husband was in the witness box.

Douglas Gordon told the court that he was an engineer, and his job required a great deal of travel. He was currently working in Cheshire but had been working in south Wales at the time of the murder. In January 1953, when his son was charged with murder, he had travelled to Belfast. He had been surprised to learn from Inspector Kennedy and Superintendent Capstick that Iain was suffering from headaches. He had not been at home for his son's 1953 new year visit, but his wife had told him that Iain seemed agitated and slept a great deal while at home, although she had not mentioned headaches. He had told Inspector Kennedy that his son had suffered from headaches in the past, but this recurrence was news to him. In general, Douglas Gordon agreed with the description his wife had given of the behaviour of their eldest son.

For the prosecution, George Hanna questioned Douglas Gordon about some letters he had received from Iain which he had handed over to Inspector Nelson on January 17,

1953. Douglas Gordon then read aloud the first letter from his son dated Sunday 16 November 1952.

After the customary greetings, the letter told how Iain had seen two films recently: Elizabeth Taylor in *The Light Fantastic* and Bette Davis in *Another Man's Poison*, and he had gone to the cinema with another person about whom he gave no information. He complained that he was getting no help with the trade examinations the RAF expected him to sit. He then told his father about Patricia Curran's murder. 'I knew the girl slightly, and the family especially her brother Desmond, so I do not feel too good.' The letter went on to say that Patricia Curran had sustained 22 wounds. 'At the inquest, I believe it was stated that she was raped, strangled and stabbed; but please do not mention that to anyone as it is unofficial.' Iain Gordon went on to tell his father that Patricia was 'the last person anyone would wish to harm', and that he was 'deeply upset and profoundly shocked'.

Douglas Gordon then read aloud his son's subsequent letter to him dated Wednesday 19 November 1952. After the usual greetings, and a gentle complaint that his father had not written to him for a while, the letter got down to business, as it were:

> As I have not been out this week so far, there is not much to tell you except for one very important thing. You remember what I said to you in my previous letter about the murder in Whiteabbey? Since then I have been interviewed by the RAF police and the RUC. Everybody was interviewed by the RAF police. On Monday, the RUC questioned me no less than three times. They were up at camp at 12am and in the afternoon, I was at Whiteabbey police barracks and there a statement was taken from me regarding my movements on Wednesday and my relationship with the Curran family. As if that was not enough,

they were up at Edenmore in the evening. This is all because I was acquainted with the family of the deceased girl and they are, I fancy, hoping that I will be able to give them a lead, but I was useless to them as I knew the girl so slightly.

The letter went to on to describe his movements on the afternoon of the murder. Iain Gordon concluded by saying: 'As far as I am concerned there is nothing at all to worry about; but I will be relieved when the killer is arrested and charged with the murder of Patricia Curran. If, of course, anything of a serious nature arises, I will notify you at once.'

Two other letters from Iain to his father were put into evidence, but no questions about them were asked. But one significant piece of Douglas Gordon's evidence passed without question.

Hanna for the prosecution: 'Did you hand those letters to the police on 17 January 1953?'

Douglas Gordon: 'Yes, on Saturday, I handed them to Inspector Nelson, I think.'

Hanna: 'The police first got them on 17 January?'

Douglas Gordon: 'Actually Detective Sergeant Hawkins had seen them in November.'

That ended Douglas Gordon's evidence.

Brenda Gordon was then recalled to vouch for a letter she had received from her son around the time of her birthday, 14 December; she thought that might have been in 1951.

Agnew then read the letter aloud.

Dear Mother

You asked me to rewrite my birthday letter to you and to drop all reference that my former one contained to religion and socialism. As it was written in a hurry, your request is quite natural and I am happy to say that I agree to it, but I do not know if I can completely delete all references to socialism and religion. However, we shall see. I cannot say what will be written. I am just going to let your pen do the writing. So, don't blame me for what is being written, but your poor pen.

The letter continues in this rambling vein, appearing to apologise but not apologising for not giving his mother a birthday present, saying that presents should be given all year round, blaming 'convention' for hindering him and others in doing what they wished to do. He gave the example of a boy and girl, strangers to each other, travelling in the same railway carriage. The boy eventually asked the girl for a kiss, to which she replied: 'It's not exactly done at the first meeting is it?'

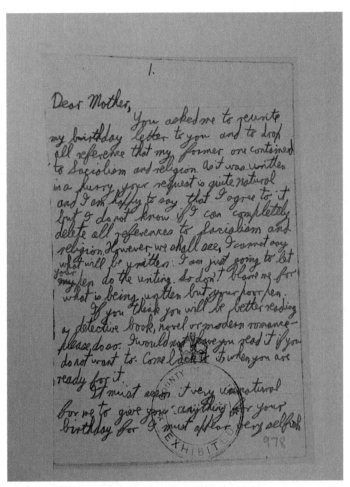

Figure 5: The first page of Gordon's confused and rambling undated letter to his mother–why the defence introduced this is hard to fathom

His letter went on to cite Victorian attitudes to dress, saying that what appeared unconventional in that era today appeared commonplace. 'In future years to be a communist will not be regarded as unconventional.'

It is hard to see why the defence would want to put such a muddled and rambling letter into evidence. Praising communism to a middle-class jury in Belfast during the Cold War did the accused no favours. And the reference to a young man wanting to kiss a young woman without her consent was bound to trouble the jury in a case involving the murder of a young woman.

Gordon's parents left the witness box without the jury learning much about the horrors they and their sons had encountered living in Asia during World War II. Burma then had been a difficult and dangerous place. It had been a British colony before the war and would gain independence afterwards. Japan invaded in 1942 because it desperately needed oil. Japan would never completely control Burma then; nor did Britain which had to deal with insurgency from emerging independence movements. For a mining engineer with a young family the fear of what Japan would do to prisoners was well-founded.

William McColl, the next defence witness, said he was a retired businessman from Scotland. He had befriended Gordon in Dollar when the boy was about nine years old. He thought of the boy as being 'peculiar', but they had struck up a friendship. When he got older, Gordon used to help in his shop on Saturdays, delivering parcels and so on. They both shared an interest in running, and he had coached Gordon for a race. About 50 yards from the finishing tape, Gordon had stopped without reason, thus throwing away the race. 'I had never seen anything like that done before; he had plenty of running left in him.'.

Squadron-Leader Edward O'Toole was then called. He told McVeigh that part of his duties included running the central registry at RAF Edenmore, and one of the clerks under his supervision was Iain Hay Gordon. He said the first thing he noticed about Gordon was that he was exceedingly keen. 'He went out of his way to assist me. He was always waiting at the door if you wanted something.' But Gordon tried the squadron-leader's patience. 'In spite of his obvious keenness, he didn't seem to be able to do anything right.'

There was another problem.

'Unlike the average airman, he was not – shall I say resilient – he couldn't take a "telling off", go away, try to do the thing properly and hope for the best for the future.'

'What way did he react?' Bertie McVeigh asked.

'He became terribly depressed and, on several occasions, he bordered on tears.'

Mistakes occurred, the squadron-leader explained. Gordon's duties involved handling incoming and outgoing mail, but he sent letters to the wrong people, lost copies, and put files put back in the wrong place almost every day. O'Toole also noticed that Gordon had no friends in camp. When he asked him why he used to spend time in the central registry after his work was done, he said he preferred to be there. He wanted to write letters. He had no privacy in the barrack room, he wasn't very friendly with anybody and had no friends to go out with.

In cross-examination, O'Toole said that he never noticed any violence from Gordon, that his promotion to leading aircraftman was routine, and that he had three times transferred Gordon out of the registry because of his poor performance, but on each occasion, he had taken him back.

The RAF camp commandant, Pilot Officer Richard Popple, took the stand. He was not in direct charge of Gordon, he said, but he was responsible for the welfare and discipline of the airmen at Edenmore. He had observed Gordon at close quarters. He confirmed much of the previous witness's testimony regarding Gordon's keenness, yet poor performance. Popple also confirmed that he had told Hawkins on 29 November and again on 13 and 14 January that if written statements were to be taken from Gordon, a witnessing officer from the RAF should be present.

During cross-examination by the prosecution, the judge intervened to ask if Popple would describe Gordon as 'a stupid man'. Popple replied: 'It is not a normal word I use, but if you were to put it into my mouth, yes, I would, I would.' He also said that he had noticed that Gordon was up and about every morning long before the other servicemen in the camp.

The next phase of the defence took a different tack. Defence witnesses so far had supported the argument that Gordon had not committed murder; the evidence about to be presented would concede that he could have committed murder without intending to do so, because of a medical condition. McVeigh's two-track strategy, referred to before, was making consistency impossible.

So, the defence called no less than five medical specialists. The first task was to explain what effect an earlier head injury Gordon had suffered might have on his subsequent behaviour.

Harold Rodgers, professor of surgery at Queen's University, Belfast, said that Gordon was admitted to the Royal Victoria Hospital in the early hours of the morning of 22 December 1951. 'He was suffering from a scalp laceration, a cut to the back of the head; that is to say, he had a cerebral contusion.' Gordon had been admitted through the outpatients' department, he said.

[Another doctor, Angus McNiven, a Scottish medical expert who did not appear at the trial, in a deposition said that Gordon told him that his head injury occurred at Tyrone House in Malone Road, Belfast. These premises were used for military training, but no further information was given. McNiven's psychiatric assessment of Gordon had been provided to the jury, along with others saying that arising from the head injury Gordon had been unconscious for about 45 minutes, and that he was kept in hospital for about 15 days between 22 December 1951 and the first week in January 1952.]

Professor Rodgers told the court that the ill-effects of a blow to the back of the head are more likely to arise from the shaking up of the jelly-like substance of the brain than from the blow itself. In reply to a question from the judge, the professor said it was impossible to say if an injury of that kind would have any long-term effects. 'But in this case, a head injury of moderate severity, I would expect quite a few people to recover completely and few not to recover, my lord.'

McVeigh then questioned the professor about rigor mortis, and the judge joined in. In summary, both wanted to know would rigor mortis hold an outstretched arm upright or would gravity pull it down to align with the recumbent body. The answer to that question is not clear from the witness's replies.

Professor Rodgers was followed by radiologist Dr. William Shepherd, also from the Royal Victoria Hospital, who said that on 13 February 1953 he found a two-inch fracture on the occipital bone at the base of Gordon's skull, and that it was still open. At that stage, Gordon was in custody on a charge of murder. Nobody asked and nobody explained how Gordon, then a 19-year-old airman, had to attend a Belfast hospital with a 'head injury of moderate severity' a few days before Christmas 1951, one which had not completely closed up when he was medically examined after his arrest for murder some 14 months later. Elsewhere Gordon claimed not to know how his head injury had happened. He thought he might have intervened to separate two other conscripts who were fighting, but he remembered nothing else, he said.

A neurological surgeon, Alex Taylor, explained that his work at the Royal Victoria Hospital involved the care of patients suffering from disease or injury of the central nervous system. His opinion was that a head injury, such as the one that Gordon sustained in December 1951, would cause some brain damage, and this might bring to the surface latent schizoid tendencies. He had studied the X-rays cited by Dr Shepherd but had never examined Gordon.

Dr. Harold Millar told the court that he had qualified as a medical doctor and was a member of the Royal College of Physicians in London. He had also been trained in electroencephalography in London. 'Electroencephalography is a means of recording the electric pulsations of the human through the skull', he said. This produced a pattern on a sheet of moving paper.

He had tested Gordon in this way, attaching sensors to his skull, on 8 February 1953 in Belfast. The result was abnormal, he said, but under cross-examination he admitted that Gordon had correctly answered questions put to him during the test to determine if he was fully conscious of his surroundings. This test had been carried out in the presence of Dr. Rossiter Lewis [who was in court and would give very significant evidence the following morning], four policemen and a technician.

For the defence McVeigh objected to the fact that police officers had been present during this process. An examination ordered by the defence had been observed by the police who were reporting back to the prosecution: 'I wish to make, as strongly as I can, a protest against such conduct. We [the defence] had to arrange to have this medical examination, to have the prisoner brought from the jail. The only way he could come was under the custody of police officers, and if the defence cannot carry out an examination without having the details of that carried to the Crown, it is a poor showing for this prisoner.' McVeigh also objected to the witness being questioned on a medical report commissioned by the defence, yet the defence had not had sight of it.

The judge disagreed. On the first count, McDermott ruled that if Crown servants were present, they could report anything relevant to the inquiry. On the second, he said he was '…in the hands of the Attorney' which appears to mean that Warnock could do as he pleased, and McVeigh could do nothing about it

Dr. Robert Blair, who said he worked in the metabolic department of the Royal Victoria Hospital, gave evidence of testing blood samples taken from Gordon and concluding that he was suffering from hypoglycaemia (low blood sugar). There were many symptoms of this disease, Blair said, including outbreaks of bad temper, becoming violent and bouts of possessing great strength. The patient would know nothing of these episodes afterwards. He would not know what he was doing at the time he did it.

On further questioning by the judge, Blair said it was 'possible' that Gordon was suffering from hypoglycaemia on 12 November 1952, but he would not put it more strongly than that.

The court adjourned for the day at 6.14pm. The jury must have been mystified. They had heard that tests had been carried out to determine Gordon's brain activity while being asked a series of anodyne questions, and that he was asked to make some simple calculations. He had answered most in a reasonably satisfactory way, but the point of all this was not made clear to the jury. To make sense of much of what they had just heard, they would have to wait for the evidence of Dr Rossiter Lewis the following day.

Saturday 6 March 1953

The first witness on the last day of the trial was a Scot, Thomas McAslan. His evidence was given, out of sequence, interrupting an otherwise coherent flow of medical evidence. It is not clear why, as McAslan said he was present in court both days.

He was a member of 2502 squadron of the Auxiliary Air Force when Gordon was briefly an orderly at Aldergrove military airport near Belfast in 1951. He also encountered Gordon at a summer training camp at Watchet, Somerset, in August 1951. Gordon had been present at that camp, and his strangeness led to him becoming the butt of practical jokes among the other servicemen. They ganged up on him, saying that he would have to pass a test of his cycling ability. Thereafter when he rode his bike around the camp there was an L plate attached to the back of the saddle.

McAslan also described mock boxing matches held in servicemen's quarters, which Gordon 'won'. Gordon did not appear to understand that he was the victim of an elaborate joke, as when his opponent fell down and feigned unconsciousness, and Gordon was acclaimed as winner. On another occasion, in the hold of a landing craft used for training, Gordon 'fought' a bout with another man, with the rest of the squadron looking on. He appeared not to notice that his opponent's black eye had been applied with boot polish, and the blood flowing copiously from his nose was red ink. 'One night I was to fight him for the title of the best fighter in the squadron – this was about midnight – I went down for two or three counts and I was eventually carried out, supposed to be unconscious, and Gordon was acclaimed as champion boxer of the squadron. Gordon seemed to take it quite seriously', McAslan said.

'I formed the view that he [Gordon] wasn't just exactly right in the same way as other people', McAslan told McVeigh. After this, there was a general feeling that the joke had gone far enough, and the mock boxing matches ceased.

The first medical witness to be called on Saturday morning pulled the second strand of the defence strategy together in a manner which appeared to satisfy most people in court. Even though within a few short years his expertise and specialty would be regarded as little short of fraudulent.

If this trial had a star witness, it was Dr. Arthur Rossiter Picton Lewis. The *Belfast Newsletter* described him as a 'consultant psychiatrist practicing in Harley Street, London'. He was best known for using drugs to uncover suppressed truths. At this time 'lie detectors' were much in vogue in criminal proceedings, and Lewis, who had worked in the prison service as a psychiatrist, and was now in private practice, was a prominent practitioner of this aspect of criminology. In this trial, which he had attended every day, he was not trying to detect lies but attempting to uncover forgotten truths, he said. Lewis had been persuaded to take on the case by Gordon's aunt Dr. Webber.

Lewis, after examining Gordon at length in Belfast expressed the opinion that he was suffering from schizophrenia and hypoglycaemia. He said he had decided – following his examination on the eighth and ninth of February 1953 – that when Patricia Curran met Gordon at the gateway to Glen House on the day of the murder, he was at the beginning of a hypoglycaemic attack. On that occasion, Lewis was able to inform the court, Patricia Curran was the first to speak. 'I have ascertained to my satisfaction that he [Gordon] did not recognise her when he was about to pass her, and for what it is worth, I think it can be taken as the beginning of a hypoglycaemic attack', Lewis said.

After exchanging some pleasantries, Patricia Curran, according to Dr. Lewis, had asked Gordon to escort her up the avenue because it was already dark. The subsequent assault at the side of the driveway, the dragging of the body into the undergrowth to the tree where the stabbing occurred, were caused by Gordon's hypoglycaemia, exacerbated by his underlying schizophrenia.

An essential part of Dr Lewis's investigation was to establish to what extent memory of a 'forgotten' incident could be restored, he claimed. He administered thiopentone, a drug then popularly known as the 'truth drug' to test this.

John Agnew asked Lewis what effect this had.

'The effect of giving this test is to restore memory for an incident which has been forgotten. If that incident did not register properly in consciousness on account of insanity, it would not, in my opinion, be possible for any memory of it to be brought back. I found that I could restore Gordon's memory for the early incidents on the grass verge, and I am of the opinion that at that particular time an assault with his fist took place, but that no knife was used then; neither was there any question of any sexual assault.'

Judge: 'Well, do you mean by that – that having applied this drug – you restored his memory for what he must have known at the time?'

Lewis: 'Yes.'

Judge: 'And that included in what he must have known at the time was an assault with the fist but not with the knife?'

Lewis: 'That is so, my lord.'

Judge: 'Well, it follows from that, if I understand your evidence correctly, that, in your opinion, he knew he hit Miss Patricia Curran with his fist when he was doing it?'

Lewis: 'Yes, my Lord.'

In this fashion, a defence witness was able to inform the court that not only was Gordon guilty of murdering Patricia Curran, but the witness, Dr. Lewis, was also able to provide details of the attack that the accused had neglected to include in his confession because he had 'forgotten' them.

Dr. Rossiter Lewis's expert opinion was that the attack on Patricia Curran could be divided into three distinct stages. In the first, Gordon assaulted her at the verge of the driveway, striking her with his fist or some implement and knocking her unconscious. The second stage consisted of dragging her into concealment in the undergrowth, probably because of the approach of the paper delivery boy, George Chambers, at around 5.45pm. The third stage was the stabbing, which Dr. Lewis thought had taken place under the tree where the body was found. He considered that Gordon had lost his memory of the first stage, but that it was restored following treatment involving the administration of thiopentone.

Dr. Lewis, went on, under cross-examination, to spell out his understanding of the relationship between schizophrenia and hypoglycaemia:

'I think that the first assault was the result of a schizophrenic outburst – an uncontrollable kind of action – from which there was some short recovery. I am of the opinion that, when he had taken the body behind the bushes to the tree, the full effect of the low blood sugar came into play and that what he did then – if it could be distinguished – was more due to hypoglycaemia than to schizophrenia; and that is why, in my opinion, he had no memory which could be restored for that particular event, namely, the actual stabbing; and my reason for saying that is that the schizophrenic sometimes does remember the details of his crime – and often quite clearly – sometimes he does not; but the hypoglycaemic, since his brain cells have been affected at the time, because of lack of sugar is unable to register what is happening; and therefore there is no proper memory for the event; and that connects with my findings under the influence of the truth drug.'

Defence counsel Agnew then asked Lewis the question which put the whole performance into context. But as he did, both the judge and the attorney-general intervened to clarify technical aspects of it. The verbatim record is lengthy and tedious Eventually Agnew's three attempts to put one question boiled down to asking the psychiatrist if Gordon was insane when he murdered Patricia Curran.

Dr. Lewis: 'I am of the opinion that he was insane at that time.'

Dr Lewis, the principal witness for the defence, was in the witness box for most of Saturday morning, being examined and cross-examined on Gordon's confession and the extent of his culpability for the actions he described in it. The prosecution tried to make a case that Dr Lewis's conclusions were not well-founded because Gordon was fasting when he had been subject to various tests, and this could have affected the results.

The lunch break was delayed allowing Lewis's contribution to conclude. When the court sat again at 2.22p.m., the prosecution called one medical witness in rebuttal. Dr. James Mulligan was resident medical superintendent of St James Hospital, Armagh. His physical examination of Gordon, carried out in February 1953, showed him to be a thin, rather unhealthy-looking, asthmatic man. He reached the conclusion that when Gordon encountered Patricia Curran and tried to kiss her, he knew what he was doing, and he knew that it was wrong. And when he tried to stifle her cries, he knew he had done wrong.

Under cross-examination, Dr. Mulligan agreed with the diagnosis of hypoglycaemia. He could not give an opinion on the effect or otherwise of Gordon's head injury on the night of the murder. Dr. Mulligan thought Gordon had schizoid tendencies but said he did not have enough evidence to diagnose schizophrenia in his case.

Asked about Gordon's birthday letter to his mother which had been read out in court, Dr Mulligan said he thought it fitted with Gordon's rather unusual personality.

He thought him suggestible, easily led, unstable and weak-willed. He went further, in response to a defence question, describing Gordon as an 'inadequate psychopath'.

The judge then put a series of questions to Dr. Mulligan. They were largely technical questions about the nature of schizophrenia and to determine if Dr. Mulligan agreed with certain points that Dr. Rossiter Lewis had made. After twenty-eight such questions, McVeigh asked the judge to desist from cross-examining the witness.

The judge replied: 'I am not cross-examining the witness: I am trying to get the facts referred to on this charge.'

McVeigh persisted, saying that the attorney general was there to put questions on behalf of the prosecution. He reminded the judge that 'there are certain indications that a judge should not take an undue part in questioning a witness after counsel have finished, and I suggest that your lordship might perhaps think that he should refrain from further questioning and leave the matter as it stands.'

The judge replied that he had not been 'asking questions against the interests of your client' but simply to help the jury. He would desist from asking further questions if that was what McVeigh wanted. McVeigh said it was.

'All right, I will desist.'

John Agnew gave the closing speech for the defence. He was on his feet for more than an hour and he argued strongly that if the jury accepted that Gordon was suffering from hypoglycaemia and was also suffering from schizophrenia at the time of the attack, then he was not in his right mind, and that 'guilty but insane' was the correct verdict.

Agnew dismissed the evidence of Mrs Lyttle that she had seen Gordon at the gates of the Glen on the evening of 12 November. She had initially been unable to pick out Gordon at the identity parade, her eventual identification of him followed publication of his photograph on the front page of the

Belfast Telegraph, a copy of which was in her house, though she claimed she had been too busy to look at it.

The judge interrupted Agnew twice, once to correct a fact: the door into the room in which Capstick and Kennedy obtained Gordon's confession was not locked, as Agnew had said. Agnew withdrew that.

A more substantial judicial interruption came when Agnew spoke of a medical witness's evidence about when Gordon had lost control. The judge took the opportunity to point out that he had been trying to clarify Dr. Mulligan's view of that when McVeigh had asked him to desist.

If Agnew was bothered by the judge's interruptions, he gave no sign of it, and when he finished around 5pm, the judge adjourned for tea.

When the court resumed twenty minutes later, George Hanna began to wind up for the prosecution. He remonstrated with the defence for attacking police evidence, and said they were trying to have it both ways. The confession, which they said had been obtained under pressure which they deplored, had become the cornerstone of their argument that Gordon was insane at the time of the murder. Hanna criticised McVeigh for making 'wholly unwarranted' attacks on Superintendent Capstick in the latter's absence.

Hanna also mentioned in passing something that has troubled those who have subsequently examined the case. Capstick had written more than 3,000 words in longhand in a relatively short space of time and presented statements on the spot for Gordon to sign. 'It takes some time to take down 3,000 words in longhand' Hanna said, but he did not pursue that point. As for the defence's contention that nothing incriminatory had been found on Gordon's person, Hanna replied that nothing had been found to connect any other person either. So much for innocent until proven guilty.

The judge then summed up the case for the jury. He told the jury that they had two questions to answer:

1. Did Iain Hay Gordon kill Patricia Curran?
2. If he did kill her, is he responsible, given his state of mind at the time?

Much of the judge's charge to the jury involved repeating what has already been reported. According to the official record, the jury retired at 8.45pm and returned with its verdict at 10.43pm. The record continues:

Clerk of the Court: 'Mr Foreman, have you agreed to your verdict?'

Foreman of the Jury: 'Yes, my Lord.'

Clerk of the Court: 'Do you find the accused guilty but insane?' Foreman of the Jury: 'Yes.'

Clerk of the Court: 'Gentlemen, is that the verdict of you all?'

Foreman: 'Yes.'

Lord Chief Justice McDermott then addressed Gordon: 'Prisoner, the jury have found you guilty but insane. The order of the court is that you be kept in strict custody until Her Majesty's pleasure be known.' This formula of words meant that Gordon would be sent to a mental hospital for an indefinite period.

McVeigh asked the judge to allow Gordon's parents to speak to him before he was taken away, and the judge agreed. The court adjourned at 10.46pm. Outside the court a crowd of about 800 clapped and cheered as the prisoner was taken away.

Dr Rossiter Lewis left the courthouse and left Belfast without speaking to Gordon's parents. There had been an almighty row over defence tactics the previous day. He had pleaded with them to allow Iain to take the stand in his own defence. Walmsley and McVeigh had opposed this vehemently and Gordon's parents had eventually backed their lawyers. Lewis felt – as the man who would save Iain Hay Gordon's neck with his dubious evidence – more attention should have been paid to his advice. Douglas and Brenda Gordon were confused and upset by this difference over tactics. They did not like the solicitor Walmsley and found the lead counsel McVeigh unsympathetic but in the end felt that they needed to back their son's defence team.

CHAPTER 3

Almost half a century lost to legal muddle and confusion

After a shocking event like the murder of Patricia Curran, nothing was ever going to be quite the same. Not for her family, nor for the man beginning an indefinite sentence in a lunatic asylum. The aftershocks form a major part of this story. But on a larger canvas, changes were afoot that would affect many lives, and some of those changes would come full circle, eventually causing Gordon's conviction to be set aside and his name cleared.

In Whiteabbey, the mill would close, and the transition from partial industrial centre to pleasant middle-class suburb would be completed. Not everyone felt the same about Whiteabbey. Journalist James Fox, writing in 1968 in the *Sunday Times*, described it as 'small, quiet, a totally characterless place, ugly, depressing and gossipy.' This was a harsh judgment; some would say too harsh.

In the immediate aftermath of Patricia Curran's murder, changes were felt. Parents became more anxious about daughters getting home on time. The policeman on patrol cast a beadier eye on strange faces appearing on his patch. Young women, fearing that they risked meeting the same fate as Patricia Curran, thought again about plans to leave home to go to college or take up a job in an unfamiliar town.

Men walking home from the bus or train late at night kept their distance from unaccompanied young women, lest their nearness would give cause for alarm. The girls they met at the tennis clubs or dances were more difficult to get to know, since they did not know whom to trust anymore. Hadn't Iain Gordon, the man convicted of stabbing Patricia Curran thirty-seven times, been a quiet and inoffensive lad until he had been afflicted by some kind of demonic possession, or so the evidence at his trial had suggested?

Fathers, mothers, brothers and older sisters became more watchful, more suspicious of any strange man who paid court to a pretty young daughter or sister. Who knows how many budding romances were stifled by this extra scrutiny? In time these effects would dwindle, but some realisation of the enormity of what had happened to a pretty nineteen-year-old in a quiet Antrim village in November 1952 would lodge in local memory for a long time.

On a larger canvas the changes following the ending of World War II were beginning to make themselves felt. In the immediate locality of Whiteabbey, the provision of 'homes fit for heroes would see a fine new town built nearby at Rathcoole; sadly that would become a hotbed of sectarian divisions. Other changes were coming too. Many of them would not start in Northern Ireland but be filtered and moderated through the link with Britain, where the pace of social, industrial and eventually legislative change, particularly in the field of human rights, was quicker.

Taking a long view, an optimistic observer might hope that, legally speaking, London would drag Belfast into the twentieth century, as Brussels would later do for Dublin, and to an extent that was what happened. For the present, Belfast's shipbuilding days continued and the Troubles – as Northern Ireland's undeclared civil war was to be called – were not even a cloud on the horizon.

Gordon's trial had lasted a week and it got saturation coverage in the Belfast newspapers and considerable coverage abroad. Then, just as quickly as the tap of publicity was turned on it was switched off. A confession – though the defence had half-heartedly challenged it, and perhaps the police had not been too squeamish about how it was obtained – tends to close down public speculation about the possible innocence of a convicted man. And that's what happened here.

After being returned to prison as a convicted murderer, Gordon would soon be on his way to a mental hospital to serve his time. The question arose–where the young man was to be held? It is fair to say that nobody was in any rush to have him. Some voices called for him to be returned to Scotland.

A newspaper headline - Antrim folk don't want Gordon at Holywell hospital - *Ballymena Weekly Telegraph* 10 April 1953, set alarm bells ringing. Holywell included a closed ward for the criminally insane.

In many ways Holywell was an ideal place for treating troubled people. The site, on the outskirts of Antrim town, consisted of a cluster of buildings, designed by Belfast's great architect Charles Lanyon, placed on a pleasant sloping campus in open countryside overlooking the north-east corner of Lough Neagh. Unlike many forbidding-looking institutions built in the nineteenth century, Holywell's peaceful surroundings provided a verdant setting for the treatment of troubled souls.

And the staff at Holywell were largely drawn from the people of the nearby town. The same family names appeared on staff lists down through generations, making for strong and supportive links between the hospital and the local community. The townspeople could be relied up to turn out in large numbers for concerts and garden parties held at

Holywell. Dances there featured in the social calendar of that part of the country and drew large crowds.

However, the hospital's management committee initially did not want Gordon. It sent a lengthy letter to the area's Hospitals Authority 'strongly disapproving of a person of this type being sent here'. The committee set out seven reasons for its opposition:

1. The exaggerated publicity given to the case would react adversely on the hospital.

2. Having a notorious murderer at Holywell would make the public regard the hospital merely as a prison and damage efforts to make the treatment of mental health problems better understood in society at large. Recent legislation was intended to convey to the public that curing people rather than punishment was the purpose of such institutions.

3. Holywell lacked facilities for keeping patients such as Gordon in close custody and apart from other patients.

4. The presence of a convicted murderer would have a depressing and demoralising effect on other patients, especially those availing of services through outpatient clinics.

5. The demoralising effect on staff, given the lack of secure accommodation. Nurses would fear being held to blame for any possible escape.

6. Having such a person at Holywell would exacerbate existing problems in recruiting and keeping staff.

7. General uneasiness in the locality about the ability of the hospital to keep Gordon under lock and key.

Initially the Hospitals Authority appeared to agree, and it raised the matter with the Northern Ireland Ministry of Health. In a reply, dated 7 August 1953, the ministry said it had seen no evidence that the work of mental hospitals was adversely affected by the presence of criminal lunatics [having been found guilty but insane, that was how Gordon was viewed] and without such evidence was not going to change its mind.[viii]

Meanwhile Gordon was at Holywell and would stay there.

Official attitudes were one thing, however. On the ground, the good sense and humanity of the people of County Antrim were beginning to come into play. At Holywell, the resident medical superintendent Dr Gilbert Smith and the chief nursing officer Donald Gilchrist had a stronger commitment to the hospital's motto 'To Comfort Always' than the management committee's letter suggested. Soon they became openly sceptical that the quiet young man in their custody was a criminal lunatic. Gordon spent just over a year in a closed wing of Holywell, where he gained the trust of staff, and was moved to an open wing where he enjoyed greater freedom of movement.

Robert Wilson worked at Holywell in 1953 when Gordon first arrived. Aged ninety in 2019, he recalled very clearly the first time he saw the young Scot:

> 'Being a plumber, I had a master key for the whole place. My work took me everywhere, fixing radiators, unblocking toilets, replacing washers on taps. The murder of Patricia Curran had been the talk of the country – there were so few murders then. We'd all read about it, discussed it, and we'd been shocked by it. One day in March or April 1953, I was told there was a plumbing problem in the observation ward. I let myself in. Someone pointed out Gordon to me. He was standing very still with his back to the wall. I had to be careful when going to the

observation ward because some of the men there could be dangerous, and I always carried a pipe wrench in case I was attacked.'

'I had no worries about Gordon from the very beginning. Straightaway I could see that he was frail, even weedy-looking, and I knew that a fit young woman like Patricia Curran would have [had] no difficulty in fighting him off.'

'I quickly realised that whatever had happened to the poor unfortunate girl, I could not see Gordon as a murderer, or a lunatic either. He was not vicious, the nurses clearly trusted him, and he was always quiet and did what he was told and gave no trouble. Over the years I got to like him. I found him a lovely fellow.'[ix]

Many patients in Holywell were assigned to outdoor work parties. Gordon's team looked after gardening and taking care of the grounds. He and his fellow patients spent many days outdoors working in the grounds or in the fields Sometimes Gordon was sent to a nearby farm to harvest crops; such outings provided ample opportunities to escape, had he been so minded.

Some patients were allowed to go to nearby Antrim town. Wilson says he recognised some whom he saw walking around the town, but he never met Gordon in town. Another witness said that towards the end of his stay, she saw Gordon on a bicycle going to town and returning to the hospital later that day. She assumed he was running errands for the staff.

Shortly before Gordon was released, Robert Wilson quit his job at Holywell to set up his own business as a building contractor. He said he was sorry to leave; for him it was a home from home. He was impressed by the care he saw given to patients in his time there: 'They were very well looked after.' Wilson thought highly of Dr. Smith, the resident medical superintendent.

In the intervening years Wilson did not doubt Gordon's innocence. He is very clear that few who worked with him in Holywell believed that the police had got the right man. 'There was a feeling that what had happened was closer to home, and the police had their hands tied dealing with the murder of a judge's daughter.' Wilson thought that local people – he still lives in the same house five miles from Antrim town where he and his late wife brought up their family – were probably influenced by the attitude of those who had known Gordon at Holywell. They had seen Gordon up close over seven years and come to know him as a quiet and timid soul. Their behaviour towards Gordon showed that they simply did not believe he was capable of murder.

Meanwhile Desmond Curran spent several months at the Moral Re-Armament headquarters in Switzerland in 1953 and invited friends to visit him there and to meet Frank Buchman, the movement's charismatic leader and founder. In 1946, some Swiss supporters of Buchman had restored a large, derelict hotel at Caux, in the mountains overlooking Montreux and Lake Geneva. It is fair to say that Moral Re-Armament played a role in mending fences between post-war France and post-war Germany, and thus contributed to the founding of what would eventually become the European Union.

In 1953 Desmond Curran's fellow student from Queen's University Stratton Mills was attending a conference in France with a friend. In response to Desmond's invitation, they both went to Caux for a few days. 'It was quite interesting, but I did not enjoy [being there] and left after three days', Stratton Mills said.

In some quarters in Northern Ireland, doubts were beginning to be expressed about Gordon's conviction. Dorothy Turtle (née Hersey), a Quaker who lived in Lisburn with her husband Jack and two sons, opposed capital punishment in principle, and this belief brought her into contact with Gordon's family. Her background was interesting. She had studied at Cambridge University in the 1920s and became a music teacher. While at Cambridge, she had been asked to join the Communist Party, considered it briefly but then refused. Had she gone ahead, she might have become the 'The First Woman' of the infamous Cambridge spy ring, along with Burgess and McLean, and we might never have heard of 'The Third Man'.

Later she studied politics at the London School of Economics and taught music at a village school outside Madras in India, and she met Gandhi twice. Psychology was also an interest. Dorothy Turtle corresponded with Carl Jung, the founder of analytical psychology, and met Alfred Adler, a disciple of Freud. She got a job teaching music at the Mount School, a Quaker school in York. Then she met Jack Turtle, her future husband, at a Quaker college in Birmingham. They went to Beirut where he taught in a Quaker school, they married, and their two sons were born. When Jack Turtle got a teaching job in the Friends' School in Lisburn in 1952, the family moved to Northern Ireland.

'My mother was always interested in politics and human rights, the United Nations and so on. The Patricia Curran murder case happened soon after we arrived and she and some other women, not all of them Quakers, took an interest in it', her son James recalled, speaking in Belfast in 2019.

Figure 6: A studio portrait of Dorothy Turtle as a young woman courtesy of her son James Turtle.

Calling for the release of Gordon was not a popular cause. Some well-meaning friends and acquaintances tried to talk Dorothy Turtle out of getting involved. Those who tried to discourage her were not all part of the establishment, but Northern Ireland being Northern Ireland 'where everyone knew everyone else', they were familiar with many of the people involved and did not wish to see her 'causing trouble' by reopening a tragic case which had appeared to have been resolved.

Dorothy Turtle's mother's maiden name was Cronin. She was an Anglican from a Co Kerry family and brought her daughter up in that faith. Dorothy's father was a Christadelphian. This group believed in the primacy of the Bible and rejected the idea of God being a trinity. He was English, and Dorothy got her interest in human rights from him.

Mrs . Turtle's interest in the plight of Gordon led to her visiting him in Holywell, sometimes bringing her elder son Henry with her. She became friendly with Brenda Gordon, Iain's mother, whom she came to know on her many visits to Ireland to visit Iain in Holywell.

A Scottish journalist, John Linklater, calculated that Brenda Gordon spent more than £3,500 on legal fees, medical specialist fees and paying for a private detective between the end of the trial in 1953 and 1957. This came out of her modest salary as a teacher.[x] In the 1960s Brenda Gordon, accompanied by Dorothy Turtle, went to Rome to ask Desmond Curran for help in clearing Iain Gordon's name, but he refused. (The reason for Curran's presence in Rome will shortly become clear.)

So far so predictable. Gordon's family was campaigning to have their son released, supported by some liberally minded middle-class people, the people who are often labelled and dismissed as 'do gooders'.

However, that label could not be applied to Stormont Unionist MP Walter William Buchanan Topping, who became Minister for Home Affairs in 1956. Getting Topping to take some interest in the case was an achievement. A barrister, he had been elected as Unionist MP for Larne in 1945 and followed Lance Curran by becoming the party's chief whip in 1947 and remained in that position until Northern Ireland Prime Minister Viscount Brookeborough appointed him to the home affairs ministry in 1956. And that appointment gave Topping responsibility for prisons. He probably was not surprised to receive, shortly after his appointment, a letter from Douglas Gordon seeking the release of his son from Holywell. The surprise lay in Topping's reaction. Topping proved willing to listen to what was said to him on Gordon's behalf.

When he had sentenced Iain Hay Gordon, Lord Justice McDermott's verdict of 'guilty but insane' had introduced an extra layer of complexity to the case. This verdict was regarded in law as being one of innocence. Gordon was innocent – his insanity had caused the crime, not any guilty intention. An innocent person needed no appeal, and the law did not provide one. Gordon was in the unenviable position of being a man who claimed to be innocent who was detained in a mental hospital and denied even the possibility of an appeal. The phrase Catch 22 was not yet current, but it fitted the situation perfectly.

With that avenue closed off, the best that could be hoped for was an early release. Gordon was detained 'at her majesty's pleasure', meaning until he was cured of whatever 'illness' had caused him to commit murder. In practical terms, that meant that Gordon could be released at any time, provided that there was clear medical evidence that he was 'cured' and would not reoffend. However, there was bound to be a strong public reaction to opening the cell door and freeing someone who had been sentenced a few short years earlier for the brutal and shocking murder of a young woman. Grasping this nettle would take political courage.

There were other considerations. The trial judge was opposed to releasing Gordon so soon. On being approached, Lord Chief Justice McDermott said that Gordon should serve at least nine years before being released. Although it was not stated in law, there was unofficial guidance, – known as 'the tariff' – for officials dealing with prisoners to be held 'at her majesty's pleasure', as the quaint phrase puts it. If 'the tariff' were applied to Gordon, he would become due for release in 1962.

And what of another senior judge Lance Curran? Most reasonable people would have understood if he objected to Gordon's release. After all the man had lost his only daughter. Lance Curran must have been consulted in some way about the prospect of Gordon's release, but no trace of that has been found.

Meanwhile Ian Gordon's parents continued to seek their son's release. First Douglas Gordon told Topping that he had discovered that the defence counsel Bertie McVeigh had threatened to withdraw from the case if he was required to cross-examine Patricia's brother Desmond whom he knew socially. This was a breach of the barristers' code of conduct, Douglas Gordon said.

Douglas Gordon lodged a petition to the Ministry of Home Affairs dated around June 1957, following up on a letter earlier that year. It set out five main points in support of the release of Iain Hay Gordon.

1. That Iain Hay Gordon had not murdered Patricia Curran.
2. That he was not, nor never had been, insane.
3. That there were serious deficiencies in the evidence offered and the way it was obtained.

4.   That the lawyers for the prosecution and the defence had not done their jobs properly.

5.   That the judge had not conducted the trial fairly.

The petition argued that there had been a most serious miscarriage of justice, and since the law permitted no appeal, the verdict should be set aside.

While the petition did not in itself achieve its stated objective, subsequent events show that the seeds of doubt had been sown among people who mattered, lawyers, politicians and civil servants. They are thought to have also included a future British Home Secretary Henry Brooke[xi], whose early political development had been influenced by working with Quakers and who was on a personal journey from being a supporter of capital punishment to eventually voting against it.

Another was Topping himself. He may have had some pressure from influential lawyers in Northern Ireland, not many in number but prominent enough to have the ear of those in power, who were uneasy about aspects of Gordon's trial. The name of another barrister – Harford Montgomery Hyde – crops up. He was then a Unionist MP for North Belfast, supporting progressive causes at Westminster including the decriminalisation of homosexuality and the abolition of capital punishment. Jeffrey Dudgeon's recent biography of Hyde shows that Ulster Unionist MPs then at Westminster had a free hand to support progressive causes. Hyde, a maverick, the 'joker in the pack' of Ulster Unionism's Westminster representation, made full use of this freedom. Eventually he was seen to have overplayed his hand on the subject of homosexual law reform and was de-selected in 1959, to be replaced by none other than Stratton Mills, then a rising star of the Unionist Party of Northern Ireland.

Hyde's dedication to the cause of homosexual law reform was not self-interest: he was married three times and bemoaned the fact that his second wife left him because he was spending too much time on politics. A prolific author, his works included a biography of Oscar Wilde. He was a distant cousin of the American writer Henry James.

Something was clearly afoot in the Ministry of Home Affairs in Belfast, and it surfaced in 1956, three years after Gordon's conviction. There is an attendance note for a meeting on 19 November 1956 about the Gordon case, predating Douglas Gordon's first letter to Topping, and a note mentioning a meeting on 3 December 1956 with a 'minute sheet' on the following day. Records in the possession of the campaign group Justice, which as we shall shortly see played a major part in clearing Gordon's name, also show that a letter was received from Douglas Gordon on 27 November 1957 with another following on 20 January 1958.

Dorothy Turtle had also contacted Topping soon after his appointment as Minister for Home Affairs in 1956. She and a group of other women, including Marie Hogg of Eglantine Terrace in south Belfast, and Brenda Deane of St Thomas's Rectory, Belfast had begun to campaign to have Gordon released. They met two officials of the Ministry of Home Affairs in Belfast in April 1958 and made submissions for Gordon's release. On a second visit to the ministry to hear the official response, the women were surprised to hear that while the official view remained that Gordon was convicted after a fair trial, even if this were not the case, he could not be released because he had, after his arrest, confessed to the murder. The confession that the men from the ministry now cited was not that obtained by Capstick and Kennedy, but one that they said Gordon made voluntarily to Reverend Sam Wylie in prison two days after being charged with murder. Wylie had also received letters from Gordon which confirmed his guilt, the officials, Mr. Hill and Mr. Dunbar, said. The women went away to digest this unexpected setback. Other women named as being supporters of Brenda Gordon include a Mrs. Moles and Mabel Campbell. William Hinds, a Unionist Stormont MP, had helped them by arranging meetings with officials.

The women had arranged to meet the officer in charge at Edenmore to see if the RAF could help in their campaign. Dorothy Turtle took her son Henry when the women's deputation went to discuss their concerns about Gordon's conviction. At Edenmore, they waited in a room for the officer who had agreed to meet them. Suddenly the door burst open and there stood Rev. Wylie who addressed the women and the boy in a threatening manner. 'Henry told me that he was very frightened by this big man [Wylie] who, speaking in a very loud voice, warned our mother and the other women not to interfere in matters of which they understood nothing', James Turtle said in 2019. 'I shall always remember my late brother's depiction of him, standing like some horrible gaunt dark figure, sort of threatening them with I don't know quite what.'

Wylie told the women that they knew nothing of the case, he had the whole story from the perpetrator's [Gordon's] mouth, but he could say no more because of his clergyman's duty to keep confessions secret. Wylie strongly advised them to drop their campaign. Gordon was reasonably comfortable in Holywell and if he behaved himself would be released in 1962, he said. However, if they succeeded in showing that he was sane, he would be sent to an ordinary prison, and that would be much harder on him

Dorothy Turtle, Brenda Gordon and Hugh Pierce, Justice's case officer, who became involved later and made it his business to meet Wylie, have left on file written accounts of Wylie's volatile mood swings and threats to them, confirming the picture painted by Henry Turtle.

When Dorothy Turtle next visited Gordon he told her that he had written to Wylie from prison seeking his help as chaplain, but that there were no damaging admissions in his letters. Dorothy Turtle's group then challenged the Ministry of Home Affairs to produce the alleged confession. Wylie continued to insist that Gordon was guilty and refused to produce letters he said he had received from Gordon which proved his guilt. He also said that the Holywell chaplain had received similar letters from Gordon: the chaplain denied this. Wylie complained that the actions of the women campaigning for Gordon's release had ruined his friendship with the Curran family. Eventually he was seen to have overplayed his hand and the authorities were no longer listening to him.

Among Dorothy Turtle's files on this case are copies of draft affidavits sworn by the three women campaigners who had met Ministry of Home Affairs officials before Gordon's release. All three stated that the first they heard of Wylie's attempts to halt Gordon's release came from the civil servants they met named Hill and Dunbar, and the suggestion of a second 'confession' took them by surprise. The affidavits read as if they were intended for use in the defence of a threatened libel action, from Wylie perhaps? Dorothy Turtle left no record of the affidavits being used in any proceedings.

At this stage Wylie was spending part of each year in ministry in Canada. A year later, in 1959, he left Northern Ireland for good. Around the same time Samuel Deveney emigrated to New Zealand. Many years later Dorothy Turtle maintained that by the end of 1959, it was clear that Gordon would soon be released, and the two men had left Northern Ireland before awkward questions could be asked of them. She thought it no coincidence that Albert Kennedy took a long pre-retirement holiday in New Zealand in 1959, and she suggested that Wylie had also visited New Zealand during the early1960s.

All this overlapped with the formation in London of an all-party group of lawyers under the name Justice to investigate serious cases of miscarriages of justice. Immediately its secretary Tom Sargant took an interest in Gordon's case. This was without doubt a very significant stepping stone on the lengthy road to Gordon clearing his name.

Justice, which became the British arm of the International Commission of Jurists, had the support of eminent lawyers, including Gerald Gardiner, who became Lord Chancellor in the Labour governments of 1964-70. Gardiner had reformist instincts and Quaker connections, and on at least two visits to Northern Ireland met Dorothy Turtle in connection with the campaign for Gordon's release. In 1957 Gordon was given a lengthy medical examination and psychological assessment at Holywell by a visiting doctor, Dr Desmond Curran (not related to the Curran family of Glen House) at the request of the Home Office, and it is reasonable to assume that this was part of a process to assess his suitability for release. A Scottish MP who had raised the question of Gordon's continued detention received a letter from the Home Office assuring him that Gordon was receiving 'appropriate treatment'. This was not true. Gordon was getting no treatment because he did not need it, the medical director of Holywell, Dr. Gilbert Smith told Hugh Pierce of Justice when he raised the matter with him. When asked why he had not raised this matter at official level, Smith replied that he was afraid that if he did so, Gordon would be sent to Crumlin Road jail. In this respect he was at one with Sam Wylie.

A two-page memo in Tom Sargant's file headed 'Document List IHG' recites almost 60 exchanges of letters, telegrams and memos between Justice and civil servants in London, Belfast and Edinburgh, and communications with Douglas and Brenda Gordon and with Dorothy Turtle. In 1959 Justice asked a leading barrister, Frederick Lawton QC, who later became a judge, along with another barrister Hugh Pierce, to prepare the case for the release of Gordon.

Lawton and Pierce met Topping in Belfast and made the point that a man who was not insane and was receiving no treatment for insanity was being detained in a lunatic asylum. It was on that visit that Pierce encountered Wylie.

Once the Wylie confession problem had gone away, Topping agreed to pursue the question of releasing him on the sanity/insanity issue.

A year later, Brian Faulkner, Topping's successor as Minister for Home Affairs, released Gordon, without officially conceding that the trial verdict was flawed. He warned those campaigning for Gordon's release that if there was any publicity, the deal was off. In the meantime, Gordon had been allowed out for short periods under the supervision of Dorothy Turtle. A warrant for Gordon's discharge from Holywell was prepared on 29 August 1960, and a telegram to that effect was sent to the secretary of the Northern Ireland Department of Home Affairs.

As Macbeth said of the murder of Duncan: 'If it were done when 'tis done, then 'twere well it were done quickly'. In September 1960, Gordon was told to pack his things and leave Holywell. He was to be known henceforth as John Gordon (the Scots Gaelic version of John is Iain or Ian), though for the purpose of his journey to Scotland his name was John Cameron. A job was waiting for him as a storeman in a warehouse in a publishing company in Glasgow, and also a small flat. His parents would 'keep an eye on him'. He was not to discuss his past with anyone, nor was he to seek a pardon. He was handed a sum of money – believed to be about £2,000.

Topping, who in the meantime had become a judge, his title was Recorder of Belfast, had not forgotten Gordon. He had contacted a friend in the William Collins publishing company in Glasgow and this had led to Gordon being taken on as a warehouseman. [Collins was known to have strong connections with military intelligence, as a glance at the membership of the board of directors shows, and perhaps there was an element of keeping an eye on Gordon in the appointment.] This is speculation. Topping's goodwill in helping Gordon to find a job is not.

And with that, the entire edifice of the case laboriously made out against Gordon by Northern Ireland's attorney general Edmond Warnock, wholesale perjury committed by police officers senior and junior led by Detective Superintendent John Capstick, Dr Rossiter Lewis's 'expert' evidence about something he could know nothing about, the jury's verdict of guilty but insane, the full might and pomp of the legal proceedings in the well-publicised trial presided over by Lord Chief Justice McDermott barely seven years earlier, all of it collapsed. Not with a bang and not even with a whimper.

And whoever had murdered Patricia Curran remained to be identified and dealt with.

In those seven years, what had changed? The passage of time had permitted a more balanced reappraisal of events. Moreover, several unconnected independent factors had come together to shake the kaleidoscope of known facts about the murder of Patricia Curran, and what emerged was a very different pattern to that revealed by the police investigation, trial and conviction.

In the immediate aftermath of Gordon's conviction, there had been three major unanswered questions.

1. How could a chaotically disorganised person like Gordon stab a young woman 37 times, with all the bloodshed that involves, then clean himself up in the space of less than two hours disposing of every shred of evidence so successfully that the largest manhunt in Northern Ireland's history could not unearth one item connecting him to murder.

2. Who had murdered Patricia Curran if – as seemed likely – Iain Hay Gordon had not?

3.   If Gordon was not mentally ill, why was he being
      detained in an asylum?

The last question was the first to be answered, because
Gordon was released. There were other questions. Gordon's
confession – was it voluntary or was it the result of bullying
by the police? Why hadn't the prosecution put John Capstick
on the stand for the jury to assess his credibility?

In addition, the police did not secure or search a
possible crime scene – Patricia Curran's bedroom – for three
days after any possible evidence could have been removed.
This was confirmed by a Ministry of Home Affairs official
to Dorothy Turtle and her friends. The seriousness of this
breach of elementary police procedure cannot be overstated.
Also, the police had not challenged the action of three
officers of the law, a judge, a barrister and a solicitor, in
moving a body showing obvious signs of rigor mortis away
from a crime scene with the acquiescence of a fourth officer
of the law, a police constable. Nor had the police questioned
Doris Curran until late December, more than a month after
her daughter was murdered. RUC Inspector Albert Kennedy
knew from the first days of the investigation that Lance
Curran was either mistaken or lying in his account of when
he knew about his daughter's movements the night she was
murdered. Why did the police not question Lance Curran
on this?

Notes in Warnock's handwriting, included with the
official trial records, clearly show his pre-trial doubts about
Judge Curran's account of how events unfolded on the night
his daughter was murdered. Lance Curran told Doreen
Davison on the phone around 1.30am that Patricia had left
Belfast on the 5pm bus to Whiteabbey but she hadn't arrived
home. This was during the phone call in which Lance Curran
asked her and her husband to come to Glen House to help
find Patricia. According to the Steele family, Lance Curran
did not phone their home looking for their son John to find

out when he had last seen Patricia in Belfast until after 2am, by which time her body had been found in the avenue. Lance Curran's friend and family solicitor Malcolm Davison was so troubled that he personally raised this discrepancy with the police during the investigation.

So, even if sloppy police work had led to this important line of inquiry not being disclosed to the defence, Northern Ireland's chief law officer, Edmond Warnock, knew about it from his pre-trial brief but did not chose to disclose it. Warnock's notes also show he was concerned by inconsistencies in the confession which Capstick and Kennedy extracted from Gordon. For example, on the supplementary brief included with the trial file held in the official archives, Warnock had analysed Gordon's confession, noting that Gordon was quite precise about details up to the point where he says he met Patricia Curran at around 5.30pm. 'Perfect up to this point, quite inconsistent with the evidence of stupidity. Now comes the wrongdoing', Warnock observed. Warnock's note went: 'What follows is vague and conditional. [Gordon says] "I forget what we talked about ... I noticed Patricia was carrying a handbag and something else I just I forget what it was', "I either held her left hand or her arm", "my hand may have touched her breast", I forget", "Probably", "I am a bit hazy", "As far as I know".'

Warnock's note questioned how Gordon could move from total recall of detail – before the murder – to uncertainty and vagueness in a matter of minutes. It was 'quite inconsistent with the evidence of stupidity', his note said. It was also a very clear indication that the person confessing had very little knowledge of how the murder happened.

However, Warnock had spotted another blatant weakness in the confession – it contained only already known facts. In confessing to the murder, Gordon added nothing that Capstick – or any intelligent observer – would not have already known. Essentially the confession consists of an admission of guilt along with a skilfully woven web of surmise deploying what facts were already known.

A previous note in Warnock's hand said – about detailed passages in Gordon's confession – 'the man who remembers all this should remember an officer's orders.'. Clearly the prosecution had not been convinced that Gordon was the sole author of the confession he signed.

The supplementary brief section of the trial file at the Public Record Office of Northern Ireland also contains a partially legible pencilled note, in writing which might be Warnock's. In it he or another official – the writing looks hurried – expresses concern about a medical examination of Gordon that would take place at the Royal Victoria Hospital in Belfast, at the request of the Gordon's defence team. This appears to refer to Dr. Rossiter Lewis, the 'expert' defence witness whose truth drug test 'confirmed' that Gordon murdered Patricia Curran, with the equally spurious qualification that he had not known what he was doing at the time. The brief contains a draft note addressed to 'Dear Minister', complaining about a doctor having access to Gordon. 'Some person has blundered quite frankly. I cannot understand why, without seeking any person's authority, a prisoner on a capital charge is provided with a defence of insanity.' The rest is barely legible, but the thrust of what survives suggests this might have allowed the defence to contend that the Ministry of Health was then convinced that Gordon was insane.

Before leaving the confession, it is worth noting that the only new fact disclosed in the confession was the knife, allegedly the murder weapon, which miraculously appeared out of Belfast Lough a few days later, and which Constable Herdman tried to link to Gordon. Locating a specific grain of sand in the Sahara Desert would have comparable credibility.

The retention of those notes in the Public Record Office of Northern Ireland suggests that concern over the verdict existed at an official level in 1953 about Gordon's conviction. The prosecution brief and notes did not form part of the trial transcript, yet they were preserved and included with it. Why? Did an archivist choose, or was he/she instructed, then or later, to preserve the additional documents for future reference?

There was something else going on.

Conservative and isolated though it was, Northern Ireland in the 1950s was not immune from liberalising forces that were coming into play in post-war Britain. There the abolition of capital punishment was already being canvassed, proposed in 1956 by a Labour MP Sidney Silverman – with the support of Montgomery Hyde. The measure was passed by the House of Commons but rejected by the House of the Lords. It was a narrow escape and the victory would be short-lived. Homosexual law reform was also coming down the tracks. The much-prized union on which the Ulster Unionist Party placed such importance, was becoming the means by which core Conservative and Unionist values were being insidiously weakened and would eventually be dismantled.

Curiously, Iain Hay Gordon's trial for murder was one of the few cases in which the Northern Ireland 'backwater' behaved better than the more enlightened, or so it was thought, mainland of the United Kingdom.

The trial of Gordon for the murder of Patricia Curran was a glaring injustice following a shocking outrage, but in one crucial way it could have been a great deal worse, as Bertie McVeigh had been only too aware. Less than two weeks before Patricia Curran was murdered, two young men, Derek Bentley and Christopher Craig broke into a warehouse in Croydon in south London. The police arrived and disturbed the intruders. Craig shot Constable Sidney Miles dead. The penalty for murder was hanging. Craig was sixteen and the law said he was too young to be hanged. Bentley, however, was nineteen and could be hanged. Though he had not fired the fatal shot, the jury found him guilty of murder, and Bentley was hanged on 13 January 1953.

The two cases were almost contemporaneous. The young men were almost the same age: Gordon was twenty at the time of the murder, Bentley was a year his junior. Gordon's life had been blighted – Bentley's was taken away. (Derek Bentley's conviction was posthumously quashed in 1998.) Abolition of the death penalty eventually took place in Britain in 1969, initially on a temporary basis, but was delayed in Northern Ireland until 1973.

In the 1950s some of Ulster's legal and political leaders read the signs. While the flaws in the process that had convicted Gordon were understood mostly by lawyers in the inner circles of Belfast's legal community, some saw a bigger picture. There are occasions when it is wiser to yield ground, rather than face total defeat. Miscarriages of justice, unless skilfully handled, could be a stone in the shoe of the precious union which kept at bay the Republic of Ireland and its anti-partitionist rhetoric.

A left-wing Labour MP for the London suburb of Hornchurch Geoffrey Bing had successfully opposed the election of a unionist Godfrey MacManaway to represent West Belfast constituency in 1950, forcing a by-election. Bing, born in Co Down, had formed a group of British MPs who were taking too much interest in government in Northern Ireland for unionist comfort. MacManaway was challenged as he was an Anglican clergyman and thus ineligible from sitting in the House of Commons. (Bing would later advise Gordon's mother Brenda on her challenge to the guilty but insane verdict.) The threat of London interference in Northern Ireland was both real and recent.

By 1960, the efforts of Douglas and Brenda Gordon with the considerable support of Tom Sargant and the campaign group Justice and of Dorothy Turtle and her friends had succeeded in getting Gordon released. The next victory, when it came, was forty years later and very few of those involved from the beginning were still alive.

Figure 7. Rev. Sam Wylie, minister of Whiteabbey Presbyterian church.

The changed times which had allowed Gordon to be returned to Scotland would also come to bear on the changing fortunes of two other central characters in the tragedy which had enveloped the people who lived in the little village of Whiteabbey. Nothing stands still, and after Patricia Curran's murder, their lives would never be the same.

Sam Wylie, the Presbyterian minister in Whiteabbey merits a closer look. Photographs show a confident and well-built man, untroubled by the demands of pulpit and congregation. His church was an impressive structure on Shore Road, and it dominated the coastline. The manse needed updating and the school would have to be rebuilt, but such matters were grist to the mill of the energetic and personable clergyman.

Wylie's duties in Whiteabbey included being a chaplain to the RAF Edenmore base, and it was he who introduced the recently arrived young conscript Iain Gordon to Desmond Curran after morning service one Sunday in 1951. This led to Desmond inviting Gordon to lunch at Glen House, where he met the judge and his wife Doris, and their other children Michael and Patricia.

Samuel James Wylie became minister at Whiteabbey Presbyterian church in 1947. Previously he had served at Glendermott in the Waterside area of Derry. A man in his middle years, he might have been expected to remain at Whiteabbey until his retirement. He had married Sarah (Sadie) McClements, and at this stage they had grown-up daughters. He took over from the Rev. William McMurray who had been first appointed in 1914, while Wylie was just leaving school.

Wylie was born in 1897, one of five brothers. The family lived at Castlereagh near Belfast. After a brief spell working in the United States, he was summoned home by his domineering mother, and qualified as a minister in Belfast and was licensed as a clergyman in 1927.

Among his Whiteabbey congregation, the Currans were an important family. The clergyman's constant companion, fund-raising, was needed to maintain the church buildings and meeting hall. New faces were appearing at Sunday services, as the number of commuters grew, and of course attendance was being augmented by national servicemen from the RAF base at Edenmore, just up the road from Whiteabbey.

Much of the pastoral care of the airmen would fall on the shoulders of the minister, but no member of his flock would leave a mark on his subsequent life and career like the lost soul who was Iain Hay Gordon from Clackmannanshire.

After Gordon had been arrested, Wylie felt that, as RAF Edenmore chaplain, he should visit him in Belfast jail. He did so. Gordon's solicitor Albert Walmsley intervened and told the prison governor not to let Wylie make any further visits. Wylie was a friend of Desmond Curran, had accepted Gordon's guilt as a fact, and in the years remaining to him in Northern Ireland would work to dissuade people like Dorothy Turtle from calling for Gordon's release.

But that lay in the future.

In 1953, just after Gordon been sent to Holywell, Wylie began a series of summer 'job swaps' with clergy colleagues in Canada which led to his moving there permanently in 1959. His first posting was Scarboro United Church in Calgary and he stayed there about five years and made a good impression. (United referred to a coming together of Presbyterian and Methodist communities) Cathy Smith, a member of the Scarboro congregation[xii] recalled her memories of him:

> 'Sam Wylie was a high energy, delightful man who must have rocked the boat for some of Scarboro's staider and/or elderly congregants. We had big congregations in those days. Mr. W. would deliver an entertaining, power-packed sermon in precisely 15 minutes — never longer — leaving any snoozers in the dust. He never used

notes or the lectern but paced back and forth at the front of the church, and spoke faster, more eloquently, and with greater wit (in his thick Irish accent) than any preacher before or since. I believe his sermons were theologically sound, but his presentation was certainly more than our dour old church was accustomed to.'

'My father was a retired minister, but he sang in the choir every week and was actively involved in church and presbytery. He admired Sam Wylie very much and within our family he was always referred to as Father Wylie.'

'When my husband, David, and I were married in 1962, the ceremony was held in the garden of my parents' home. My father married us but because he had no church of his own at the time, and the union had to be officially recorded on Scarboro's books, and because we were fond of Sam Wylie, he was asked to assist with the ceremony. Mr. W. waxed most poetic about the beautiful setting under the arms of the spreading rowan tree.'

Here's another account of Wylie in action at a college graduation ceremony in Scarboro in 1960:

'The traditional dignity of graduation and the Irish wit of a United Church clergyman provided contrasts in mood for the 49th graduation of Mount Royal College Friday afternoon in Central United Church. Rev. S. J. Wylie, pastor of Scarboro United Church, provided both humour and wisdom in his address to the graduating classes; the former when he regaled the audience with anecdotes about his experiences with words, and the latter in advice for living.'

Another member of the Scarboro congregation was less enthusiastic about the Irish minister. Speaking in 2017, she recalled him being somewhat 'theatrical' saying that he delivered very intense sermons but then would see the time on the clock at the back of the church and stop abruptly, sometimes in mid-sentence. And she described making a visit to Ireland and deciding to visit Wylie's church in Whiteabbey. She was asked to sign the guest book and must have written something about being from Scarboro in Calgary and mentioned that Mr. Wylie had been the minister in her church for a time. Apparently, she spelled his name wrongly and a church 'elder' noticed. Then he said never mind, perhaps it's just as well. He told her that Wylie had made the congregation build a 'big new manse for him, and then he left'. He made it clear that Wylie was not too popular in Whiteabbey.

Sam Wylie left Scarboro about 1964. He briefly returned home when his wife Sadie was in her final illness. She had initially accompanied him to Canada but soon returned to Northern Ireland to live with a married daughter and son-in-law and their children.

Wylie's next lengthy posting was at First United Church, Dawson Creek, British Columbia, a mining town, as the name suggest. He took up duty in November 1967. Again, he told the congregation to expect 15-minute sermons and gave notice that as a bachelor, which he now effectively was, he was a poor cook and expected to be invited to put his feet under every family's table. In that way he got to know everybody, he said, because he had met them all at dinner in their homes. He was careful not to outstay his welcome, always leaving at 7.30pm, thanking his host and hostess, saying he had letters to write.

An official history of the church[xiii] described him as 'Calgary's silver-tongued orator' and recalled his accommodating Catholic services at First United when a neighbouring church burned down. This was ecumenism of a high order and would hardly have been possible in Ulster. Wylie was still stationed in Dawson Creek when conflict on the streets of Belfast and Derry made worldwide news. He asked his congregation to pray for an end to the violence. He left Dawson Creek in 1974 to go back to Calgary.

Accounts of Wylie's Canadian ministry show him playing the stage Irish card. 'The top of the morning to you' was how he greeted members of his congregations, and he told them that the expected response was: 'The rest of the day to yourself, Reverend'. He gave church services to mark St Patrick's Day and King William's famous victory at the Battle of the Boyne on 12 July.

Wylie's Irish blessing is featured in the congregation's official history: 'May the road rise up with you, may the wind always blow at your back, may the sun shine warm upon your face, the rains fall soft upon your fields and, until we meet again, may God hold you in the hollow of his hand.'

A niece, Trish Wylie, who lives in Northern Ireland, had not known that she had an uncle who was a minister of religion in Canada until 2010 when she began to compile a family tree. She found that he was the second of five sons, and outlived all his brothers, including her father. A sister had died before Sam was born, and this loss weighed heavily on his mother, a very religious person who was active in the temperance movement, and it seems likely that it was her influence that led to her second son becoming a clergyman.

At the age of seventy-seven, he returned to Calgary. A Presbyterian publication in Northern Ireland noted his death in 1992.

Wylie's leaving of Whiteabbey, and his subsequent lifelong exile, was clearly evidence of guilt over his role in what had happened to Iain Gordon. Be that as it may, in his late fifties he was also energised by the challenges of ministry in the wide-open spaces of western Canada, and he made a vivid and lasting impression on his new congregations. His journey could now be measured in more than miles.

What of the Curran family during all this? Immediately following Patricia's murder, Lance and Doris, Desmond and Michael had moved to 7 Deramore Drive, south Belfast, later moving a short distance to 19 Deramore Park which became the family home. In 1956 Lance became a Lord Justice of Appeal. In the intervening years, if he had any thoughts on the progress of Iain Gordon's attempts to clear his name, he kept them to himself, or within the confines of the Ulster Reform Club in Belfast where he continued to enjoy a game of poker.

Desmond became a Catholic in 1957 at a ceremony in Clonard Monastery, Belfast. He had earlier stopped working as a barrister. This caused a rift between father and son, and Desmond moved out of the family home to stay with a friend called Michael Sherry in north Belfast.

Coincidentally Michael Sherry was a close friend of Kathleen Magowan, the daughter of Minnie Magowan, murdered by 'Robert the Painter', whom Lance Curran had unsuccessfully prosecuted as attorney general. Desmond attended a going-away party for Kathleen, when she eventually found she could no longer live in Belfast after her mother's death, especially with the murderer, Robert Taylor, at liberty.

In the meantime, the public had been alerted to a potential miscarriage of justice . In 1958, a British Sunday newspaper reporter got access to Glen House, to which the Curran family had never returned after their daughter's death. On lifting a carpet in what had been Patricia's bedroom, Duncan Webb of *The People* newspaper found a large dark stain. He contrived to remove some pieces of floorboard for analysis, but the results were inconclusive – the stain could have been caused by bloodstains or but also by varnish. Fitted carpets were not the norm then. The perimeter of a room was often treated with wood stain and varnish if a carpet stopped six or eight inches short of the wall, and a spillage of stain on the floor hidden by the carpet could not be ruled out.

A unionist MP called on the Northern Ireland government to hold an official inquiry 'to dispel once and for all the gossip which exists', and a nationalist senator called for an immediate ban on imported newspapers! Duncan Webb's inconclusive scoop did not resolve matters, but it did put the case back on the agenda. Webb – who believed in Gordon's innocence – was a colourful character in an era when Fleet Street crime reporters often sailed close to the wind. He had been alerted to the case by a private detective called Kenneth Leach. Leach did much detailed investigatory work, tracking down fellow conscripts all over the UK, but became exasperated by Gordon's refusal to admit having had sex with Desmond Curran.

Also in 1958 Desmond Curran went to Nigeria for two years to work as a lay teacher for a Catholic organisation St Patrick's Missionary Society. He taught at St Thomas teacher training college, Ogoja. At that time, many lay teachers taught in schools alongside missionary priests. Their salaries were paid by the Nigerian government.

In early 1960 Curran taught at Glenstal Abbey for a short while, and he may have been considering joining the Benedictine Order which ran the boys' boarding school in County Limerick. There he was advised that he should seek a more active ministry and was admitted to Birmingham Oratory. Later in 1960 he went to the Beda College in Rome to study for the priesthood, and he was ordained as a priest for the archdiocese of Cape Town on 14 March 1964. This was also a significant year for Lance Curran, first because he attended his eldest son's ordination, and later that year

Lance was knighted by Queen Elizabeth II. The decision to attend Desmond's ordination must have been difficult. In doing so, he went against what might be called his tribal allegiances, but he was reconciled with Desmond and that must have meant much to both men.

Meanwhile in 1961 Lance Curran had presided over the trial of Robert McGladdery for the murder of nineteen-year-old Pearl Gamble, near Newry. McGladdery protested his innocence but was found guilty and was hanged at Crumlin Road jail, in Belfast, on 20 December 1961. Lance Curran thus entered the history books as the judge who pronounced Northern Ireland's last death sentence. At this remove it seems unwise judicially, and also personally insensitive, to ask a man whose nineteen-year-old daughter had been brutally murdered to handle a trial that was bound to revive ghastly memories.

Ten years later, two more major milestones were passed. In 1974 Lance Curran retired from the bench and he and Doris celebrated their fiftieth wedding anniversary. About six months later Doris suffered a stroke, from which she never fully recovered. She died on 29 May 1975. Her address at the time of her death was given as Malone Road, rather than Deramore Park. This is because she died in a nursing home, just around the corner from the family home. She died without leaving a will. Letters of administration for her estate of £5,645 were sought later in 1975. Curiously the date of her death is given as 1972 on a headstone in Drumbeg churchyard.

Some commentary on Doris's life after Patricia died suggest she was laid low by grief and was thereafter house-bound or confined to a mental hospital. However, I have also heard accounts of her attending social events with her family in later years. She spent her last years in south Belfast, living quietly with her husband and with a nurse companion who looked after her. Speculation appeared on internet sites about her mental state in the years after Patricia was murdered, including a claim that she spent her childhood living in a mental hospital. The known facts do not support this. Her father, James Lee, originally from Blessington, County Wicklow, was the resident superintendent of a reformatory for boys in south Belfast, and a misunderstanding of the nature of this institution may account for suggestions that Doris had been brought up in a mental hospital.

Figure 8: Memorial stone in Drumbeg graveyard for members of Curran family. Doris died in 1975 not 1972.

In 1976 Lance Curran married his sister-in-law Peggy, Mrs Margaret Pearce Curran (née Blair), the widow of his late brother Gerald. Lance and Peggy lived in the south of England at Rushlake Green, Heathfield, East Sussex, Lance Curran died, aged 85, in 1984 around the time that Glen House was sold. After a high security funeral service at Drumbeg parish church, on 26 October 1984, he was buried in the family plot where Doris and Patricia and other members of the family are laid to rest. His funeral took place in dangerous times. Heavy security was on hand to protect Lord Chief Justice Lowry and other eminent lawyers and senior policemen, all of whom were potential targets for the IRA. The Brighton hotel bombing of the Conservative Party conference had occurred just a couple of weeks earlier. Prime minister Margaret Thatcher was fortunate to escape, five were killed, and others maimed or injured. Earlier in the year, the IRA had killed three British soldiers and two RUC men in Northern Ireland in two attacks on 18 May.

'Legal dignitaries started arriving at the church at around 10.30am. They were driven to the door in a fleet of armoured Ford Granada cars', the *Belfast Telegraph* told its readers. The tiny church was packed to overflowing when the service began at 11am with a reading from Father Desmond Curran. Family members present included Lance Curran's second wife, Peggy and his son Michael. The service was conducted by Church of Ireland minister Rev. Cecil Clarke who bade the congregation to give thanks for Lance Curran's long and distinguished career. The sound of running engines in the armoured cars at the back of church, ready for a quick getaway in case of trouble, could be heard throughout the service. The pews were packed with bulky bodyguards and security men, and vehicle checkpoints were in place within a half-mile radius of the church.

Tributes to Lord Curran were led in Belfast High Court by the Lord Chief Justice, Lord Lowry. In the costive vocabulary affected by legal bigwigs of the time, Lancelot Curran was truly an ornament to his profession, he said. 'Of anything counterfeit or pretentious he was the avowed and effective enemy, but of that which was good and honourable, he was a friend and ally.' Lowry went on to say that in and out of court Curran had the gift of 'tolerating human failing while at the same time keeping control of the major issues.' Lowry was clearly referring to difficulties with colleagues when he said that Curran was his own man and incapable of any devious action. 'When he disagreed or disapproved, he did so openly and nearly always amicably. But he reserved his wrath for what he saw as being morally wrong or corrupt. When he was engaged in this way, he was formidable indeed.'

After the service, Lance Curran was laid to rest in the adjoining graveyard. His life's journey had been lengthy and difficult. As a young man he was an officer in the Royal Flying Corps, which became the Royal Air Force in 1918, during his service. An older brother Herbert had been killed in northern France on 17 May 1916, serving with the Royal Fusiliers. He was twenty-one years old. Herbert Curran is buried at Pas-de-Calais and is commemorated in a plaque at Elmwood Presbyterian church. After war ended, Lance enrolled at Queen's University, Belfast and had been awarded a Bachelor of Arts degree in 1921 and was called to the Bar two years later. In 1924, he married Doris Lee, known to her family as Dorrie. According to *Who's Who,* he lectured in law at Queen's University during World War II, with the rank of major in the British Army. In 1945, he was elected to the Stormont parliament representing the Carrick division, and was attorney general from 1947 to 1949, when he became a judge of the High Court, being promoted to Lord Justice of Appeal in 1956. He retired in 1975.

He had been successful in politics and in law, and as a judge was well-regarded by his peers. Lance Curran was seen as a good judge of facts, but as a lawyer he was not in the 'first eleven', according to a legal colleague who did not wish to be named. But the tragic death of his daughter and the circumstances in which it happened, in which his own role was open to very serious questions, cast a long shadow which he never shook off. Although born into a staunch Presbyterian family, he had married Doris in a Methodist church, and was laid to rest in the rites of the Church of

Ireland, with the participation of his eldest son, Desmond, a Catholic missionary.

In his will Lance left a considerable sum of money to his second wife Peggy, and his interest in a house called Rock Cottage to Michael and his wife, with smaller bequests for his grandchildren, Michael's children, and his second wife's children. (Despite its name, Rock Cottage was a substantial house in which Michael and his family lived, close to Drumbeg churchyard and the town of Lisburn.) Lance Curran must once have hoped that Desmond, with his first in classics at Cambridge and a law degree from Queen's University, would follow in his legal footsteps. Instead Desmond had become a Catholic missionary involved in the anti-apartheid movement in South Africa. He had participated in the activities of the United Democratic Front which came to the fore in the 1980s. Desmond Curran helped Professor Henrik van den Meurwe to arrange talks between the then still-banned African National Congress (ANC) and Afrikaner academics and progressives. Van den Meurwe was an important 'fixer' in the anti-apartheid movement. This was an important stepping stone on the road to the release of Nelson Mandela in 1990.

Curran's vocation lay in the slums of Cape Town where he chose to live and die. He lived among the poor with few creature comforts. There's a glimpse into his life in Kayleshita, an impoverished and lawless black township of Cape Town, in a memoir by Gerry Lorriman, his friend and fellow priest:

> I now do all my own cooking, including Sunday supper for Des Curran, parish priest of the neighbouring black township. Des, a Cambridge classicist and successful barrister before becoming a priest, and I had some interesting times during the State of Emergency. We led mass funerals and gave evidence against

the Riot Police and the Army in the Supreme Court.

Once we were water-cannoned and arrested. When I remarked to the policeman, who finally discharged us with a warning, that their water cannon was not as powerful as all that (though it just about knocked you flat), he replied: 'Well it's like this, Reverend. We don't like to use too much force against a frail old man like you. Have a good day, Reverend.'

Des and I used to go to the nuns on a Sunday evening for supper and TV. Now that they have gone, and neither of us has a TV, he comes just for a meal and a chat. One thing that is essential for our health, happiness and contentment is apple pie. Not long after the release from prison of Nelson Mandela and the end of the state of emergency, a series of ferocious township taxi wars broke out in various places in South Africa. Many taxi drivers, owners and passengers were killed. One day a teenage parishioner was coming home from Cape Town in a taxi on the main N2 highway. Another taxi drew alongside and opened fire, a bullet grazing the back of her neck. An infinitesimal difference in relative speeds and she would have been killed or left quadriplegic.

On another day, with much violence around, the father of a young man, a taxi owner, climbed over the wall and asked me to get him away quickly, as a colleague had just phoned him to say that the opposition were on their way to kill him. Simultaneously my phone rang – Nthuseng, our parish council chairperson – to say her children had phoned to say that two houses were burning nearby. Could I go around and, if necessary, bring the children back to the church? She and her family were under threat from the opposite direction because her husband had been a [rival] driver. The fugitive's plight seemed more urgent, so I drove him to friends at the far end of Gugulethu, thence to Nthuseng's house in New Crossroads. Her own mother was with the children, and there seemed no imminent threat, so they decided to stay and phone me if necessary. By the time I got back to the church, the opposition had already been and shot down the fugitive's neighbour, also a taxi driver. [This account is taken from a Jesuit publication, undated. Gerry Lorriman SJ died aged 96 in 2011.]

Neither Gerry Lorriman nor Desmond Curran were in the usual mode of missionary priests. Lorriman had also taken a circuitous route to holy orders. He had been married and had grown up children when his wife died and he joined the Jesuit order. Both were educated men with ample opportunities to live comfortable lives. Instead, they chose to live and die amongst the poorest of the poor. Curran had been living in a converted shipping container with just a bed, a table and a chair for furniture. His parishioners in Kayleshita called him Isabane - 'The Lamp'.

REMEMBER

Fr Desmond Lancelot Edward Curran

Archdiocese of Cape Town

Born: 27 August 1926
Ordained: 14 March 1964
Died: 20 August 2015

*"All I ask is that you will remember me
at the Altar of the Lord."*

Figure 9: A memorial card for Demond Curran, courtesy of Archdiocese of Cape Town archives.

Meanwhile Desmond's younger brother lived in Northern Ireland. Michael, sometimes known as Myles or Miles, was a businessman. The Curran brothers were very different people. Desmond was an intellectual and seeker after eternal truths, Michael preferred to get on with practical matters. Desmond preached total abstinence from alcohol; Michael enjoyed a social drink. Desmond lived, ate and slept as his impoverished flock did. Michael enjoyed his creature comforts. Records of past pupils at King William College, Isle of Man, describe his career thus: 'Chartered auctioneer and estate agent. International property developer – Australia, Middle East, Europe, UK and Eire'. The reality was more prosaic. He had prospered as an estate agent, and branched out into property development, losing a great deal of money in the process.

Michael married a GP, Dr Florence Smyth, and they had four children. Michael died of cancer in 1991 and is buried at Drumbeg along with his widow Florence, known as Flop, who died in a car accident in 2008.

CHAPTER 4

London eventually takes the lead

A pattern can be detected in the way the UK political and legal system handled the wrongful conviction of Iain Gordon. After the flurry of activity which led to Northern Ireland minister of home affairs Topping and his successor Faulkner releasing Gordon in 1960, the pattern moved to one where London did the pushing with Belfast resisting further steps to right this miscarriage of justice.

Iain Gordon probably did not see the connection, but nine years after he began working as a storeman in a Glasgow publisher's warehouse, rioting in the Bogside district of Derry pushed his campaign for a pardon up the agenda. The ensuing deployment of British troops called into question the very existence of the Northern Ireland system of law and order which had dealt so harshly with him. Classified secret documents, subsequently made available, disclose an intriguing picture of civil servants thinking ahead of developments unfolding on the streets of Northern Ireland.

The process of London having to take a closer interest in Northern Ireland affairs had begun at least a year earlier. From the start of civil rights demonstrations in 1968, the authority of the Northern Ireland government was being eroded. In London, the Home Office established a separate Northern Ireland division in 1969. When direct rule from

London was imposed in 1972, this unit would become the Northern Ireland Office with its own secretary of state at the cabinet table in Westminster.

In 1964 the Labour Party, led by Harold Wilson, had narrowly won the British general election and increased its majority at an election in 1966. This meant that the Unionist Party had lost an important ally in government in Westminster. The nationalist community in Northern Ireland saw the Labour ministers, if not as natural allies, as being well-disposed. And as we've seen Gordon's supporters had an influential ally in Wilson's government, the Lord Chancellor, Gerald Gardiner.

In October 1969, when Harold Wilson spoke at a public meeting at St. Mungo's hall in Glasgow, Gordon approached him and asked him to help him clear his name. He told the prime minister that he had been framed by two Scotland Yard detectives and held in a mental asylum even though the staff understood that he was sane. Wilson asked Gordon to write to him, setting out the facts of his case. In fact, Gordon, or more likely Justice acting on his behalf, had written to Harold Wilson much earlier, in August 1966, seeking a pardon in the following terms:

1. His confession to the murder was extracted when he was in a state of collapse after continuous questioning.
2. In 1955, the Northern Ireland government was presented with further evidence but would not consider reopening the case.
3. In 1958, the matter was referred to Justice, the British section of the International Commission of Jurists.
4. In August 1960, following representations to the Northern Ireland government, Iain Gordon was released, but there was no admission of a miscarriage of justice.

5. The superintendent of the mental hospital where Gordon was detained said he had never found any evidence of insanity.

Wilson's 1966 reply to Justice, compiled for him by the civil service in London, said that the administration of justice in Northern Ireland was the responsibility of the Stormont government under the Government of Ireland Act 1920, and so he could not intervene. This was the 'official line' adopted by whomever was in power at Westminster when problems arose with Stormont's version of justice. It also meant that when Labour MPs at Westminster with heavy concentrations of Irish voters in their constituencies tried to raise allegations of 'gerrymandering' in Northern Ireland elections, they were ruled out of order. The election of a socialist republican, Gerry Fitt as MP for West Belfast in 1966, who voted with Wilson's Labour Party, allowed him a platform to criticise unionism at Westminster, with the help of Labour MPs representing constituencies with predominantly Irish electorates. There was some appetite for this among Irish voters in Britain. Wilson's own constituency of Huyton, near Liverpool, contained a strong Irish contingent.

The Glasgow public meeting came after the Northern Ireland troubles had started, and the dispatch of British troops to patrol the streets of Northern Ireland. In November 1969, the knotty question of how Wilson should reply to Gordon in the light of Britain assuming *de facto* responsibility for law and order in Northern Ireland, once again engaged minds in London and Belfast. A little over a month later a civil servant in London wrote to an official at Stormont, enclosing Gordon's letter to the prime minister and seeking his view on how the matter should be handled. Wilson had promised Gordon that he would look into the matter and write to him. Gordon's was not the only such problem troubling the mandarins. In considering other cases involving nationalists complaining of discrimination by the RUC and the courts, a British Home Office official D.B.E Hopkins wrote:

> On the one hand, they are matters for the government of Northern Ireland under the Government of Ireland Act, 1920, but on the other hand they are matters to which in current circumstances it is difficult either for the prime minister [Harold Wilson] or the home secretary [James Callaghan] to reply that they are not matters of their concern.

'Current circumstances' referred to the deployment of the British army on the streets of Northern Ireland on August 14, 1969, following three nights and two days of rioting in the Bogside of Derry, and other centres. The Northern Ireland government had lost control of what was happening on the streets, and the British government had stepped in and taken control and could now be held responsible. Earlier in 1969, a reform-minded Unionist prime minister Captain Terence O'Neill had been forced to make way for his more hardline cousin Major James Chichester-Clark. Direct rule from London would not come until 1972, but the writing was on the wall, and the civil service knew that.

Hopkins's letter asked H. Black, a senior Stormont official, 'for your views, in sufficient detail to construct a reply to Mr. Gordon'. He also mentioned the detention of three brothers called Hamill from Dungannon, 'on which Fr. Denis Faul, a priest with nationalist sympathies, and a Labour MP Eric Moonman had been campaigning. Unstated but understood was the fact that Moonman, a prominent left-winger, was someone Wilson needed to keep on side.

Another item in the Northern Ireland file is a lengthy internal memo addressed to Hopkins, clearly intended to encourage Stormont officials to understand that change was coming down the track: 'I think it would be helpful if Mr North, you and I joined together to draw up some form of guidance for the department [Home Office] as a whole. Clearly our relationship with the Northern Ireland government is different since August, but it is a matter of knowing how far this change reflects the manner in which we should deal with individual matters put to us that are within the competence of the Northern Ireland authorities', wrote P.K. Leyshon.

That memo from London, headed 'Northern Ireland Complaints about Administration of Justice' and addressed to Hopkins, begins thus: 'The considerable publicity given to Northern Ireland affairs over recent months and the "reformist" attitude of the British government towards Stormont has led to a number of cases which can only be described as complaints against the administration of justice in Northern Ireland.'

Leyshon said his immediate concern was how to deal with petitions for clemency, requests to nullify a conviction or reduce a sentence. He suggested some administrative measures, but it is clear that the most pressing problem was how a senior minister, or the prime minister, should best reply when asked to respond to an alleged miscarriage of justice while no longer being able to hide behind the Government of Ireland Act, 1920.

The memorandum cited three cases in which the actions of the Northern Ireland judiciary were under the spotlight, one being that of Gordon. In this case there was the added complication that the reply drafted for Harold Wilson in 1966 no longer applied. What could he, should he, now say in his reply? It mentions Gordon's claim to Wilson that 'some eminent persons, including the present Lord Chancellor [Gerald Gardiner] and Attorney General [Sir Elwyn Jones] believe in my innocence.' Both were senior members of Wilson's Labour government. Leyshon then poses the question: 'Would it do the cause of Northern Ireland any good if the [Gordon] case were reopened?'

This is hardly the best test to be applied where a miscarriage of justice is at least a possibility, but something else stands out. Barely three months after the 'Battle of the Bogside' on television news bulletins all over the world showed RUC men in Derry batoning unarmed civil rights demonstrators, senior civil servants in London understood that there was something seriously wrong with the administration of justice in Northern Ireland and were drawing up plans for the day when Westminster would have to take responsibility .

And here we can see the quiet behind-the-scenes work of Justice. The organisation's mission statement, though it did not then use such terminology, said: 'Our vision is of fair, accessible and efficient legal processes, in which the individual's rights are protected, and which reflect the country's [Britain's] international reputation for upholding and promoting the rule of law.' There is more than a whiff of post-colonial jingoism here, though its denigrators would always regard Justice as a left-of-centre stalking horse. Gerald Gardiner described the advocacy group as 'the conscience of the legal profession'.

The first director of Justice, Tom Sargant, had asked his nephew-in-law, a lawyer called Hugh Pierce, to take on Gordon's file in 1958, and his mastery of the case helped to bring about Gordon's release in 1960. Pierce would die in 1988 before Gordon's appeal was eventually heard. Note that nowhere did Justice argue that Gordon was innocent. It concentrated on one narrow front. Gordon had been detained because he was thought to be insane. By showing that he wasn't insane, he was released. (Brenda Gordon gave credit for this focused approach to Geoffrey Bing but he lost his seat in parliament in 1955 and went abroad. In effect, Bing's legal work for the Gordon family was taken on by Hugh Pierce.)

That left the conviction. Gordon had been convicted on the basis of a forced confession and other irregularities. Again, Justice would focus on one simple angle: the legal shortcomings of the confession. The broader argument about whether Gordon was guilty, or innocent was for others to make. His conviction could be set aside if an appeal court could be convinced that irregularities undermined the conviction. But the road to the appeal court was blocked by two enormous legislative hurdles. The first required changing the law affecting all potential miscarriage of justice cases. When that was eventually cleared, another emerged from nowhere which applied to just one case – that of Iain Hay Gordon.

By way of explanation, the tortuous legal proceedings arose in the following way. In Britain in the 1980s and 1990s politicians and senior lawyers had realised that the appeals court procedure was not working. Clear cases of miscarriages of justice, the Birmingham Six, the Guildford Four and others, were not being dealt with in a timely or satisfactory matter. The answer was to set up a statutory body, the Criminal Cases Review Commission (CCRC), which began work in 1997. It acted as a clearing house for appeals, subjecting them to a preliminary investigation, and where a strong case could be shown to exist, referring it on to the appeal court.

Now to get a miscarriage of justice on to the CCRC docket as it were, you first needed an advocacy group like Justice to do the legwork. So, there was a conveyor belt system for handling miscarriages of justice. In the first stage you sought the support of a group such as Justice which was staffed by lawyers. If Justice thought the case had merit, it made a submission to the CCRC. In turn, if the CCRC was persuaded, it activated the third stage by referring the case on to the appeal court. This all took time, and the unfortunate victim of the alleged miscarriage of justice remained convicted throughout.

None of this was made easy. In 1992 a senior RUC officer assured Henry Turtle that the original police investigation files were not to be found, nor could the Public Record Office help with the trial records. This assertion that no records existed of a high-profile murder trial was not true, but it shows how the establishment was obstructing the course of justice. By 1995 Gordon was already in his sixties, and though at liberty his life had been blighted since 1953 when he had just turned twenty-one.

Justice did its bit, analysing the flaws in Gordon's conviction, assembling expert witnesses to back his case. However, the CCRC did not accept Gordon's case, stating that its remit did not include 'guilty but insane' verdicts which, as explained earlier, were regarded as technical acquittals.

On being challenged about this, the CCRC referred the case to the Northern Ireland Court of Appeal. Despite Justice's high profile civil rights lawyer Sir Louis Blom-Cooper's submission – that the new verdict 'not guilty by reason of insanity' (which *is* within the CCRC's remit, and which had replaced 'guilty but insane' verdict in recent cases) – was to all intents and purposes similar, the Northern Ireland Appeal Court endorsed the CCRC's refusal to consider the case.

An amendment to the Criminal Appeal Act 1995 was now urgently required to fix this Catch-22 situation. In July 1998 Lord Ackner introduced a private members' Bill in the House of Lords with such an amendment.

Lord Williams of Mostyn gave what was needed – an acceptance by the British government that the law required amendment. Ackner had support from Home Office civil servants in the drafting of the Criminal Cases Review (Insanity) Bill and its explanatory notes. Williams spoke again in support in the Lords and gave his support throughout. Their names are mentioned here to show that not all lawyers exist in a bubble of their procedures and privilege. Labour's Chris Mullin MP, champion of many unpopular Irish causes, put his shoulder to the wheel in the House of Commons, but it took until 1997 to clear the road for Gordon's appeal to be heard, which culminated in Belfast in 2000.

Public interest had been whetted once again when Gordon and Curran were reunited in a sunny outdoor setting in the summer of 1995, BBC Northern Ireland broadcast two documentary programmes examining the murder of Patricia Curran.[xiv] A publicity photograph showed two late middle-aged men sitting on a sunlit park bench during one of Curran's visits home. Gordon is speaking and gesturing with his hands while Curran is listening.

On screen, Gordon greeted the priest as if meeting an old friend, acknowledging his work for the oppressed in Africa and asking him to consider speaking up in his favour because he too had suffered from discrimination. This was Gordon's cack-handed way of saying to the priest, 'I didn't murder your sister, and you know that. Now, please say something to help me to get a pardon', but being Gordon, he couldn't say it out straight.

Curran knew well what was intended and replied that he would consider what Gordon had said and would let him know. That part of the exchange was over in seconds. There is something disquieting about watching film of this encounter. Gordon's words are unexceptional, but his manner is obsequious, almost fawning. He had good reason to be much firmer with his erstwhile friend.

Figure 10: Desmond Curran and Iain Hay Gordon in 1995 during the filming of a TV documentary (BBC publicity photograph).

It is an unfortunate fact of this case that Gordon's general demeanour was unimpressive. He was the sort of man that only his mother could find it in her heart to love, as the saying has it. He comes across in the few pieces of film that exist of him as needy, anxious to please and also curiously self-satisfied, if that makes sense. A Scottish journalist, John Linklater, who had helped Gordon's legal team to prepare the appeal, and observed him over a period of time, noted that Gordon was pathetically grateful for any attention, even when that attention came about as a result of him being in trouble. How much of that was a consequence of the years of suffering visited on him for a crime he did not commit, there is no knowing.

Here Gordon was wasting his time. Desmond Curran, while studying in for the priesthood in Rome, had refused a similar request from Brenda Gordon. Desmond Curran's considered response to Iain Hay Gordon, when it came, was negative. On reflection, he still believed that Gordon had murdered his sister, he said, but said accepted that he might sincerely believe that he had not. God would forgive him. The court verdict was correct, Curran maintained. He continued his hostility to Gordon's cause, even after the appeal court had lifted the conviction, Curran then said that while he accepted the appeal verdict, it lacked meaning unless it identified the person who had committed the murder. This was a cheap shot from Curran who had studied law and knew that was not how courts of appeal worked. And of course he also knew who had killed his sister.

The TV programme also showed Desmond Curran preaching to his flock in a tin s church at Khayelshita, an impoverished shanty town near Cape Town, South Africa. He comes across as a good man and a dedicated pastor, living the simple lifestyle of his black African flock, and much loved by them. As he aged ,he grew in stature; gone is the gauche young man who thought Moral Re-Armament would save the world. In photographs of the young Desmond Curran, his prominent ears catch the eye. Now he has filled out and they have somehow become less obvious, as he has gained in authority. His accent has a slight white South African timbre as he tells his flock: 'You must forgive what has been done to you by the oppressors in the past, just as I have forgiven the man who murdered my sister Patricia many years ago.'

Richard Popple, who attended Gordon's trial on behalf of the RAF, told the BBC programme-makers that he might have witnessed a different kind of conspiracy. In his view, it occurred after the halfway stage in the trial when the defence had lost the argument to have the confession ruled out of order. Defence counsel Bertie McVeigh had abandoned his previous stance that there was no evidence to link Gordon to the murder, and was now pinning his hopes on a medical defence, arguing that if Gordon had carried out the murder, he was so unwell at the time that he didn't know what he was doing. Popple was amazed:

> 'I'm not saying there was direct collusion, but I was astounded when I heard the psychiatrist expert witness for the prosecution and the psychiatrist for the defence saying almost the same thing, as if they were reading from the same script. I was astonished to hear two expert witnesses who were ostensibly opposed to each other both seeming to go for the same result.'

Popple, the RAF officer in charge when Gordon was at Edenmore, had been promoted to wing commander when he spoke to a BBC reporter in 1995. Popple added that when news of Gordon's arrest for the murder had first reached the RAF at Edenmore camp, the reaction was incredulity. Nobody – neither officers nor men – believed him capable of murder. Even at that early stage some of the RAF officers feared that he had been forced into confessing, Popple said.

The BBC programme producer, Bruce Batten, said: 'We spent eighteen months investigating all aspects of the case and travelled to Scotland and South Africa to carry out interviews.'[xv] A subsequent history of the BBC in Northern Ireland claimed that the broadcast 'spurred Stranraer solicitor Margot Harvey, by then Gordon's solicitor, into action. She saw thousands of documents which opened up an entirely new interpretation of the night of the murder.'

It seems more likely that Margot Harvey's skilful exploitation of the thousands of documents in the RUC files which became available to her in the 1990s as the appeal process swung into action had begun before the TV documentary. Her work, along with the earlier legal groundwork of Hugh Pierce of Justice, and the investigative skills of journalist John Linklater came together then to deliver what Gordon had so long sought.

Margot Harvey, when offered an opportunity to comment in 2019, declined. The documents to which she gained access are closed once again. The Police Service of Northern Ireland – successor to the Royal Ulster Constabulary – refuses to allow researchers to see them, saying the murder inquiry into Patricia Curran's death remains open. If the PSNI has made any progress in investigating the murder of Patricia Curran, it is not saying. The files were opened to Gordon's lawyers before the appeal, but when the appeal had succeeded, astonishingly, they were closed again.

It would take a satirist of the calibre of Joseph Heller to do justice to this application of Catch 22. 'When you don't need to see the documents because we have a conviction, they will be open. When the conviction is set aside and you want to see how this miscarriage of justice happened you cannot see the documents.' Captain Yossarian of the United States Air Force would understand.

CHAPTER 5

Vindication comes too late

An *Irish Times* headline on 21 July 2000 read: 47-year-old murder case for appeal. You really have to read that again to understand what was going on. It had taken almost a half a century to get a simple appeal into court to be heard. Finally the CCRC had managed to send the case to the appeal court. Gordon was quoted: 'I have had so many setbacks and false dawns, but this development is fantastic news.'

At a hearing of the Northern Ireland Court of Appeal in Belfast on 19 September 2000, a report by a medical expert was quoted saying that in his view Gordon's confession was false. This was the report by Dr Desmond Curran who had first examined Gordon in 1957 in Holywell hospital.

The appeal opened on 24 October 2000 with Gordon's lead barrister Sir Louis Blom-Cooper's 'blistering attack' on the behaviour of Superintendent John Capstick of Scotland Yard, according to reporter Martin Cowley. The next day it was almost all over. The three-man court of appeal judges, led by Lord Chief Justice Sir Robert Carswell, sitting with Sir Anthony Campbell and Mr. Brian Kerr, said they would allow the appeal and give their reasons later. Sir Louis Blom-Cooper asked the court to end his client's agony there and then by pronouncing him not guilty, but Carswell said he would have to wait for the written judgment.

The detailed judgment was published on 20 December 2000. A cynic would say that was a good time for the law to admit it was wrong, when public attention was diverted by Christmas festivities. The words 'not guilty' that Gordon had so long wanted to hear were not contained in it. He had to settle for the conclusion of the three eminent judges: 'We therefore allow the appeal and quash the finding of guilt.'

The judgment is interesting on how the three judges arrived at their decision. It runs to about 50 A4 pages, the first half dealing with legal proceedings to date, before going into a lengthy summary of the known facts.

But the real meat lies in the second half of the judgment. The Crown had decided to not to put forward the confession; without the confession, there was no case against Gordon. The Crown had recognised that flogging a dead horse defending the way in which Capstick forced Gordon to confess was a waste of time. Its counsel, Ronald Weatherup QC, told the appeal court it was withdrawing the confession.

That was game, set and match to Gordon's side.

The appeal court could have left it there, by simply saying that without the confession there could be no conviction. Nevertheless, their lordships had an appeal before them, and they were going to consider it, regardless of what the prosecution did or said. To expedite the process, the court had earlier ruled that it would consider written submissions rather than hear new witnesses in person. Consideration of the grounds of appeal began with an observation from the bench that the written grounds submitted 'were voluminous and multifarious, but those argued by Sir Louis Blom-Cooper QC and Mr John Larkin (for Gordon's side) at the hearing before us may be grouped into four categories.'

1. The confession should not have been admitted in evidence.
2. The confession was unreliable and should not have been accepted as true.

3. The evidence linking Gordon with the crime was unreliable, especially regarding Patricia Curran's time of death.
4. The irregularities of procedure, allied to defects in the judge's summing-up, were such as to make the trial unfair.

The appeal court had examined expert reports supporting Gordon's plea. In summary, Professor Gisli Guðjónsson, a leading authority on false confessions, had testified in writing that the confession obtained by Capstick was not dictated by Gordon as the trial court had been told. It was the result of bullying interviewing techniques and a clever process of breaking down the witness. As Capstick had said of Gordon: 'He was broken on masturbation.' A professor of forensic psychology at King's College, London, Professor Guðjónsson's evidence had been vital in overturning the Birmingham Six, Guildford Four and Judith Ward convictions. Professor Michael Koppleman had agreed with his colleague Guðjónsson. A former Northern Ireland state pathologist Professor Jack Crane cast doubt on the time of Patricia Curran's death as originally calculated by Dr. Albert Wells, suggesting that it could have happened later at a time when Gordon was known to be at Edenmore camp. A handwriting expert, Brian Craythorn, testified that his analysis showed that attorney general Edmond Warnock *had* made the notes on the prosecution brief questioning the timing of Lance Curran's calls to the Steele household.

This confirmed that Warnock had good reasons to suspect that Lance Curran was lying about what he knew about Patricia's return home on the night she was murdered, and that he had ignored the obvious implications for the case against Iain Hay Gordon.

The appeal court upheld other criticisms of the original prosecution. The evidence of the Steele family about the timing of Lance Curran's phone calls should have been disclosed to the defence but was not. The fact that Marcella Devlin had been questioned might have been relevant to the defence but was not disclosed; that too was an irregularity. Since the confession had been withdrawn, collapsing the conviction, the appeal court did not have to rule on the effects of non-disclosure and did not do so.

On the confession itself, the appeal court considered if it should have been admitted and came to the following conclusion:

> If the appellant had not been questioned at length about his sexual proclivities on the morning of 15 January, he would not have been so ready to make the confession after lunch that day. We think that the effect on his will to stay silent is likely to have been substantial, and that the fear of having his sexual activities revealed to his family and the world is likely to have affected his mind. We therefore could not regard the confession as having been proved to be voluntary in the eyes of the law. It seems to us doubtful whether it could have properly been so regarded in 1953, for the same common law was applicable. But now that the law has been more clearly developed, we have no hesitation in saying that the admission of the confession cannot be sustained on the application of modern standards.

Apart from some criticism of Lord Chief Justice McDermott for not warning the jury about the dangers inherent in accepting identification evidence, such as that of Mrs Hetty Lyttle, and his all too obvious endorsement of the evidence of Mrs Mary Jackson, that was largely that.

The appeal court dealt speedily with the case when it finally came before it, but the manner of its disposal of the case is open to criticism. Lord Justice Carswell's observation that too much time had passed for a retrial to be feasible, with its inference that another trial might have resulted in a conviction of Iain Gordon, lacked grace, some observers noted. And the judgment contained no expression of regret that it had taken almost 50 years to bring to court about an appeal against conviction, a basic human right in any civilised country, regardless of the outcome.

Nor did the judgement indicate any concern about the protracted plight of a vulnerable man trapped by the cogs of a mighty machine, the apparatus of law and order of the United Kingdom of Great Britain and Northern Ireland.

Gordon was paid £600,000 in compensation; that award was not part of the appeal court verdict. Sadly Dorothy Turtle did not live to see Gordon vindicated. She had left Ireland in 1972. While teaching at a Quaker school in Lisburn she began getting threats. She also become convinced that the phone at the family home was being tapped by the police, or the British Army. She and her husband Jack decided to move their family to the north of England. Given what we now know about widespread covert surveillance in Northern Ireland that fear may have been well-founded.

Dorothy Turtle was not a pushover; not easily scared. She had worked as a teacher in the Middle East, she spoke fearlessly to ministers, soldiers and civil servants, but nonetheless she concluded that her family would be safer elsewhere. She is almost forgotten now but in her 20 years in Ireland, from 1952 to 1972, she did good works and supported the weak and vulnerable. On a personal level, she helped Brenda Gordon in her struggle to obtain for her vulnerable and trouble-prone son Iain. Her help was practical too: among her personal effects was a receipt for £6 for posting Gordon's personal effects after him back to Scotland when he was suddenly released from Holywell in 1960. Other Quakers, along with decent people of other faiths and none, supported her, but the noisy clamour of insurrection and terrorism have obscured traces of their quiet persistence. Dorothy Turtle died in 1986. Her elder son Henry remained in touch with Iain Hay Gordon for the rest of his life.

After the success of the appeal, two principal questions remained. What really had happened during the three days of intensive interrogation at Whiteabbey. Some clarification of that comes from Dorothy Turtle's file. The second was who had killed Patricia Curran if Gordon had not.

To answer the first. Capstick had his eye on Gordon as a possible suspect from early on. He could see that the young man was vulnerable, and he worked on that. At his encounter with Gordon in early December, Capstick first asked him about sexual matters, indecency and homosexuality, according to a lengthy statement in Mrs Turtle's possession. Gordon wrote the statement shortly after being sent to Holywell. Someone there had advised him to get it all down on paper while it was still fresh in his mind:

> 'Capstick said over and over again, had I taken a walk down to the village again, perhaps I had left a bundle of sticks behind a wall or perhaps I was out for a walk and went behind a wall to urinate and saw Patricia Curran going up a drive?'

Later that month when Gordon met Desmond Curran in Belfast just before going home to Scotland for the New Year, Capstick had further reason to be interested in Gordon. Now he was getting information about the young man not just from the RUC man Sam Deveney, Curran's friend, but from Sam Wylie, Gordon's padre. Capstick heard from Wylie that Gordon was worried about the police questioning him, and that he was pleading with Wylie to put in a good word for him with the police.

Even Patricia Curran had commented on Wylie's propensity for going over the top. 'He would be all right if he could control his emotions. He's always letting them run away with him', she said to Gordon on one of his visits to Glen House for Sunday lunch.

Going back to December 1952, Gordon's Holywell statement recalled him asking Wylie if he should meet Desmond Curran to repay the money that he owed him. 'He nearly fell over himself in this enthusiasm for me to see Desmond again', Gordon said later. As we have seen the two met at a café in Belfast and set out on a three-hour perambulation around the city. The prosecution made much of this encounter to suggest Gordon's guilt, and the defence did little to counter it by pointing out that Curran had produced the written record of that encounter. In that record Curran claimed that Gordon told him that he carried a knife in case he was attacked.

Curran's statement to Deveney told Capstick that he was afraid that Gordon was about to kill him. The notion is ludicrous. Short of Gordon producing a pistol and shooting him at point-blank range, Curran was in more danger from the old ladies with walking sticks they had passed on their way into the hostel lobby. He was a well-built, well-nourished fit man about six feet tall. Gordon was a skinny and timid five feet eight inches.

Curran maintained that their three-hour circuit of the south city was about finding a quiet place to talk. It is more likely that they were looking for somewhere to have sex. In his note recording for the police what happened between them, Curran carefully stitched in questions from Gordon about the manner of Patricia's death, the number of blows and so on. Gordon said afterwards that Curran gave a distorted account of their encounter, and that Curran was the one who first mentioned the murder and continued talking to him about details of how it happened.

Gordon also said that a letter Desmond Curran wrote him in early January 1953 had the truth of the matter (whatever secret they had been discussing), but the police took it from him when they arrested him and never returned it. Curran named Wesley Courtney – with whom both men had sexual encounters – in that letter. Gordon hoped Curran would not mention Courtney to the police, lest he implicate himself. He was partially wrong on that point. Curran told Capstick about Gordon's assignations with Courtney but not his own. Iain Gordon did not give evidence at his trial, because his counsel Bertie McVeigh knew that he would make a poor witness in his own account, so Desmond Curran's lies went unanswered.

Courtney later told a private detective later that he had information that would clear Gordon's name, but he wanted money for it. The amount demanded was high, because if he admitted having sex with men, he would risk a prison sentence. Nobody was willing to pay what he demanded. Courtney died in London of an apparent heart attack in 1964; he had been working there as a minor civil servant.

Continuing his account of the misadventures that had befallen him, Gordon said that shortly after he returned to Edenmore having been in Scotland for Hogmanay, he met Wylie who told him: 'I believe the police are getting ready to make an arrest and if it is God's will it is all to the good.' The following day Gordon was told to report for questioning on 13 January. How did Wyllie know this? Here in action is the Desmond Curran – Sam Wylie – Samuel Deveney link entrapping Gordon.

Gordon continued to insist that the police were lying about the number of hours spent interrogating him over three days. On the second day his interrogation began just after 9am and he didn't get back to camp – a matter of minutes away – until 7.45pm. Policemen came in and out of the interrogation room, shouting at him to tell the truth; he was damned and would go to hell. In the afternoon of the second day when he admitted that his alibi was a lie, the pace and pressure increased. 'I didn't want my mother to know about my life in Belfast and would have done anything to prevent her finding out.'

One of his tormentors Head Constable Russell 'stood right beside me, standing up and raising his fists over my head and waving his arms all over the place. He shouted and my head was splitting and spinning. The room seemed to be going around one way and I seemed to be going around the other. The noise seemed to vibrate all around me and back off the wall … there was a million voices coming back at me off the wall. I felt if I didn't confess, I wouldn't have a chance and would be hanged and go to hell.'

Gordon's account of the final day of the interrogation is worth considering. First thing that day, Capstick saw Gordon alone. He told him he was a sick boy and, playing on Gordon's unworldliness, promised him that he would get him first class treatment for venereal disease. This is the first mention of VD in this case. Capstick said that if Gordon confessed to the murder he could go home and see a doctor. 'Your parents and friends will never know about it because you're over sixteen. You did it in a blackout; you're not a bad boy. If you confess, you will be allowed to go home a free man and none of your past life will come out.'

It was now only a matter of time before Gordon broke. He had been caught out lying repeatedly about his alibi, and he had been humiliated over his sexual history. He had been threatened with exposure as a homosexual, and he could be thrown out of the RAF and sent to jail for that. He had been made promises – *just confess and you'll be released* – that could never be kept. Gordon was under increasing pressure for three consecutive days. He was beyond breaking point and would agree to anything. Now was the time to seal the deal.

But Gordon couldn't confess to something he hadn't done. How could he describe committing a murder someone else had done? Capstick could help with that. With pencil poised, Capstick posed a series of notional questions. 'What would have happened if you'd met Miss Curran [getting off the bus at Whiteabbey]? Would you offer to see her home? Would you ask her for a kiss?'

Gordon replied: 'Probably.'

So Capstick wrote down the 'confession'. When Gordon replied 'Probably', it went down as a statement. 'Would you ask her for a kiss?' became 'I asked her for a kiss' and so on. Gordon said Kennedy entered the room while this was going on and made no objection to Capstick's line of questioning.

The law clearly states that there can be no questions asked when an accused is giving a voluntary statement. The only questions permitted are those clarifying unclear details such as dates and times. Kennedy, who later rose to be inspector general of the RUC, swore an oath saying that Gordon's confession was a voluntary statement. That was perjury, plain and simple.

'The confession brought up no new evidence, which must be rare in criminal history, and it contained all the facts known to the police', observed reporter James Fox writing in the *Sunday Times* in 1968.

It also glided over anything resembling reality.

What do we now know about events in and around Glen House, on the outskirts of the village of Whiteabbey County Antrim, on the evening of Wednesday, 12 November 1952?

A twenty-year-old RAF conscript had taken mail from Edenmore camp to the post office in Whiteabbey village, collected evening papers from the newsagents and took them back to the base, getting there around 5pm.

Patricia Curran took the 5pm bus from Belfast's Smithfield bus station to Whiteabbey village, getting there about 5.20pm and was last seen outside the gate to the avenue which led up through the trees to Glen House. She was seen there by two witnesses, both children, George Chambers on his newspaper delivery round, and Sophie McNeice who lived in the village and was friendly with Patricia, as were many local children, Sophie was about 10 and said that she and her friends often played in the Glen. In fact when her pet monkey died a few years earlier, her father buried it in the Glen, without the Currans knowing. Outside the gate lodge Sophie greeted her in her normal fashion.

'Hi Trish – are you waiting for your brother?'

Patricia said yes, she was waiting for a lift up the avenue.

Sometime later, with no lift in prospect, Patricia began to walk up the avenue through the trees in the dark. She arrived home without incident. Her mother, Doris Curran was not at home. She was playing cards with her friend Doreen Davison at her home in Greenisland. Doris drove home sometime around 6pm. Soon afterwards the two women, mother and daughter, had words. Doris, like many mothers of teenage daughters – and probably with some justification – complained that Patricia treated her home as a hotel and never did any housework. Patricia and her mother had a volatile relationship at the time. Doris disapproved of her daughter's lifestyle – driving a contractor's van was not a ladylike occupation. Nor did she approve of her daughter working on building sites with a rough crowd, and sometimes going out to pubs and dances.

She may well have blown a gasket on finding her daughter at home, changing to go out again, discarded clothes everywhere, the house in chaos. In anger Doris reached for a candlestick and lunged at Patricia with it and struck her. Patricia staggered back and collapsed. Thinking perhaps that the girl was feigning unconsciousness to further provoke her, Doris lost control, and picking up a kitchen knife, stabbed her over and over again. By then Patricia was fading into unconsciousness . She revived enough to try to fight off her mother, but her life was ebbing away.

At about 7pm, Doris Curran phoned her husband at his club and asked him to return home immediately, which he did, getting there about 7.30pm. Patricia was dead or dying when Doris rang the Ulster Reform Club. Neither Lance Curran nor Frank Stephenson, the taxi driver who drove him home, noticed Patricia's yellow beret or textbooks on the verge of the avenue where they were found later. After leaving the judge home, the taxi driver saw a car coming from the direction of Glen House at speed towards the city. Stephenson, his curiosity aroused, managed to keep up with the suspect vehicle as far as North Queen Street but then lost it. One car driving faster than another means little but having the skills to shake off a professional driver in pursuit is a different matter. That car and driver played some part in the murder.

Desmond Curran claimed he arrived home at about 9pm and that his parents told him that Patricia wasn't back yet, and that Michael was staying in Belfast. However by 9pm the clean up operation was well under way. Wylie had been summoned away from the cricket club meeting nearby to help. The clean-up operation was thoroughly professional in its execution, and for that Lance Curran and his son Desmond have to be the prime suspects. It was not a job for a distraught mother, nor a catastrophically disorganised man-child like Gordon. Dorothy Turtle told British home secretary James Callaghan in 1969 that she and her group were satisfied that Wylie had been summoned to Glen House on the night of the murder and took part in the clean-up operation. She also said that Lance Curran had contacted RUC inspector general Sir Richard Pim in the hours following the murder of his daughter, and that the inclusion of Desmond Curran's friend Deveney at the heart of the RUC investigation team where the body was found was not a coincidence.[xvi]

Under cover of darkness Patricia's body was carried from Glen House to the side of the avenue where it could be 'found' probably at first light. The house was built into a sloping site. The upstairs bedrooms at the back were accessible from ground level. A body could be removed through an upstairs back bedroom window. The folder containing her books was still in Glen House where she had put it down on her return from Belfast. Later it would be moved to the avenue, but that was after the body had been 'discovered' – otherwise it would have been seen by those who came and went up and down the avenue between 6pm and 2am.

At this point it was essential to maintain the fiction that Patricia was still expected to come home. The last bus from Belfast came and went and Patricia was not on it. Nor was she on the last train to stop at Whiteabbey. Around 1.45am, Lance Curran began to make phone calls looking for news of his missing daughter including one to the police to check if any accidents had been reported. There was another problem. At Glen House Doris Curran becoming agitated and this would culminate with her phone call to Whiteabbey police station at about 1.50am that brought Constable Rutherford on his bike to investigate. Had Doris been sedated it is possible that the body might not have been 'discovered' until morning. But once the police knew Patricia was dead, Lance's call to John Steele's home became necessary, even though the timing was askew.

The haste in removing Patricia's body to Dr Wilson's house suggest that the plan put in place was beginning to fray at the edges. At this point it is safe to say that blaming anyone else was not even considered. People would conclude that she had been attacked in the grounds of her home by some random villain. Gordon's attention-seeking in identifying himself to the RAF police as a friend of the Curran family came as a gift from the gods to Lance and Desmond Curran and their fellow conspirators.

The timing of Lance Curran's calls to the Steele home, asking John when he had last seen Patricia, prompted Kennedy to suspect that Patricia had in fact returned home earlier that evening. He notified his superior officer Sir Richard Pim that there was a problem, a very delicate one. A possibility existed that Patricia actually returned home, and the Currans were fabricating a story to conceal the fact that she was murdered in her own home. Pim was in a very tight corner. The buck stopped with him. Nobody must know about his exchange with Lance Curran earlier on the evening of her death. Kennedy could be relied on to delay any investigation of the Curran home for now. Summoning the 'heavies' from Scotland Yard would be the next line of defence.

Strip away all the lies and perjury and what is left is just this. Patricia Curran was murdered at home on the night of 12 November 1952 following a row which flared up with her mother Doris who lost control and lashed out at her repeatedly. Her father, her mother, and her elder brother, a barrister who would become a Catholic priest, were – at the very least – accessories to her murder, as was the Presbyterian minister Sam Wylie who helped to clean up and insisted on Gordon's guilt for the rest of his time in Northern Ireland.

That the Curran family and friends closed ranks after an evening of unimaginable horror is somehow understandable and, on some level forgivable in the circumstances of a mother in a moment of madness murdering her only daughter. The involvement of some members of the Curran family in the subsequent conspiracy which entrapped Iain Hay Gordon is not.

In the days and weeks that followed the murder, the conspiracy took shape. There was a large element of chance, but changing circumstances were opportunistically bent to the common purpose of diverting suspicion from Doris Curran. Gordon's foolish attention-seeking identifying himself as being a close friend of Desmond Curran must have come as a gift to those who wanted to conceal the truth.

Take the court case. The transcript bears mute witness to the pace at which the trial judge, Lord Chief Justice McDermott, drove proceedings. Monday, the first day was given over largely to opening statements and procedural matters; only two witnesses were heard in the late afternoon. Tuesday morning was busy with evidence from those who saw Patricia Curran catching the bus to Whiteabbey and what followed. After lunch, the jury was sent away while the judge heard arguments about the admissibility of the confession and so McDermott allowed the confession to be read in the presence of the jury. More than a day's full hearing before the jury was thus lost.

On Thursday morning, the trial finally got under way and the first week in March was almost gone. McDermott kept his foot on the accelerator procedurally. When Bertie McVeigh objected to prosecution witnesses being heard out of chronological order because it made the case difficult for the jury to follow, the judge told him sharply to get on with it.

Additionally, at the end of significant pieces of testimony, a pattern had emerged. McDermott took over interrogating key witnesses, as if the prosecution had in some way 'missed a trick", or to neutralise a telling point made by the defence. For the defence McVeigh had to tackle the judge head-on over the most glaring example. In his interrogation of Dr. Mulligan over his description of Gordon as an inadequate psychopath the judge asked the doctor twenty-eight questions in quick succession before McVeigh managed to stop him. McDermott's court sat from Monday morning to after ten o'clock on Saturday night, when the weary jury brought in its verdict.

But by then a much bigger problem was facing judge, prosecution and defence, particularly the defence. At first, Bertie McVeigh and John Agnew had done a decent job of planting doubt in the jury's minds and there was at least a possibility that Gordon would be acquitted. However once the confession was admitted, a guilty verdict was inevitable. And Gordon would hang. Hanging a British serviceman in Belfast on uncorroborated confession evidence could have very unfortunate consequences. It was bound to invite unwelcome attention from do-gooders and busybodies on the UK mainland.

Besides, within the small legal community of Northern Ireland, the penny had dropped. The attorney general Warnock had a prosecution to run, but we know he had his doubts, particularly about Gordon's capacity to carry out this murder and to cover his tracks so well. Meanwhile the gossip mill at the Bar was suggesting that the case against Gordon was not as watertight as it seemed. Some wondered if the RUC had been instructed not to look too closely at the family, especially as Doris Curran was thought to be bit 'fragile', and Desmond Curran, though clearly bright, was thought to be an odd fish.

By Thursday morning, halfway through the trial, the die was cast. Whether Bertie McVeigh 'had a word' or sent his junior John Agnew to think out loud among his peers, or if that even needed to be done, we don't know. But the way ahead was clear. The defence would admit that Gordon, if he did murder Patricia Curran did so in some kind of fit, and the prosecution would not contest that seriously. The judge would go along with that, and the jury would get the message, delivered with preposterous self-confidence by Dr. Rossiter Lewis. A verdict of 'guilty but insane', would ensue and the problem of what to do with Gordon could be kicked into the long grass of Holywell Asylum, from which he was released without fuss some seven years later.

Opponents of capital punishment acknowledge that Northern Ireland's legal system – despite dreadful lapses – acquitted itself better in dealing with Gordon than English courts of the time, when innocent men Timothy Evans in 1950 and Derek Bentley in 1953 were hanged and had to be pardoned posthumously.

There is a very great irony in the fact that Gordon's trial for murder was dominated by the evidence of two charlatans. A policeman's outrageous perjury – that of Superintendent John Capstick – almost sent Gordon to the gallows. In a twist of plot which many fiction writers would avoid because it was incredible, Dr. Rossiter Lewis's equally preposterous perjury uncovering a 'forgotten memory' of something which never happened and presenting it as expert medical testimony undoubtedly saved Gordon's neck.

Epilogue

Figure 12: Memorial stone feature for Patricia Curran in Drumbeg churchyard, near Lisburn.

Patricia Curran lies buried in a family plot in Drumbeg churchyard, Co Down, about five miles south of Belfast. The setting is pleasingly rural, enclosed by green fields and mature woodlands, despite its closeness to the city. The steeple of St Patrick's Anglican church stands sentinel. The church was built in 1798, a year in which Catholics and Protestants united briefly to try to oust the British from Ireland. In nearby Saintfield, the United Irishmen, as the rebels were called, won a famous victory, but their cause was lost. Visitors to the church usually approach via the old lych gate, a handsome landmark built in 1878 in memory of a long-deceased parishioner.

The church stands on the highest part of the site; below are carefully tended rows of graves and headstones. Here you will find the Curran family plot. A carved black marble plaque records the names and years of birth and death of those buried there. Two of the three children of Lance and Doris Curran, Michael and Patricia, lie with their parents in Drumbeg. Patricia's death is also commemorated by an adjoining stone feature. Desmond Curran was buried in Cape Town in 2015.

Gordon's life had been destroyed. After his release from Holywell he lived in a modest flat and worked as a warehouseman in Glasgow. He occasionally came to police notice for minor offences. His mother Brenda wore herself out trying to get him acquitted of murder. By the time his conviction was set aside in late 2000, both his parents were dead. He had a good sum of money, repaid his supporters who had given him loans to tide him over and spent some time in Spain, but the damage was done. His life was blighted, and no amount of money could undo that.

Lance Curran kept his silence. His only recorded remark on the murder was that the law had taken its course. Doris Curran disappeared from view, only seen by her family and immediate neighbours. Like Desmond Curran,

Sam Wylie sought redemption as a minister of religion, choosing western Canada where he was well received. Of the immediate Curran family, Michael, Patricia's other brother, appeared to live the life he might reasonably expected though he lost both his wife and daughter in separate tragic road accidents.

And all this waste and destruction began with a simple row between mother and daughter which arose because Doris who was afraid that her lovely bright and stubborn 19-year-old daughter Patricia was getting in with a bad crowd.

Chronology

13 November 1952

In the early hours of the morning the body of Patricia Curran aged nineteen, a university student and the daughter of a judge, was discovered in the grounds of the family home in Whiteabbey, near Belfast. She had been stabbed thirty-seven times. Later that day personnel at the nearby RAF base at Edenmore were asked to account for their movements by military police.

15 November 1952

The RUC questioned a Scottish RAF conscript, Iain Hay Gordon, aged twenty, about his movements around 6pm on the day before the murder victim was found. Gordon had an alibi, but he admitted that he knew the Curran family socially and had visited their home.

20 November 1952

Two Scotland Yard detectives were sent to Belfast to assist the RUC in its investigation of Patricia Curran's murder.

13 January 1953

Three days of intensive interrogation of Gordon by a succession of police officers began. Initially he denied any knowledge of the murder, but he eventually conceded that his alibi was a fiction.

15 January 1953

Gordon admitted that he had murdered Patricia Curran during a psychotic episode. He was charged with murder.

2 March 1953

The trial of Gordon for the murder of Patricia Curran began in Belfast. He pleaded not guilty. His confession formed the centrepiece of the prosecution's case.

8 March 1953

The jury brought in a verdict of guilty but insane. Lord Chief Justice McDermott committed Gordon to be held indefinitely 'at her majesty's pleasure'. Three weeks later Gordon was sent to Holywell Asylum near Antrim town.

November 1956

Gordon's father Douglas wrote to the Ministry of Home Affairs in Belfast stating that his son was innocent and not insane and criticising the conduct of the trial.

June 1957

A petition affirming their son's innocence and calling for his release was sent to the Governor-General of Northern Ireland, on behalf of Douglas and Brenda Gordon. Around the same time an all-party law reform group in London calling itself Justice was formed in London. In Northern Ireland a respected Quaker, Dorothy Turtle, who campaigned for Gordon's release, became an associate member of Justice. At her suggestion, Justice took an interest in his case.

September 1960

Gordon was released from Holywell. He was advised to go to Glasgow where a job and a flat awaited him, to change his name to John Gordon and not to campaign against his conviction.

October 1969

British prime minister Harold Wilson addressed a public meeting in Glasgow. Gordon was present and spoke to him afterwards, saying that he was a victim of a miscarriage of justice.

24 March 1972

The Unionist-dominated parliament at Stormont was suspended and Britain took full control of Northern Ireland. The advice that civil servants had earlier given to prime ministers that the alleged miscarriage of justice was a matter for Stormont, and not for Westminster, no longer held.

20 December 2000

Northern Ireland Court of Criminal Appeal set aside Gordon's conviction, 47 years after he had been found guilty of the murder of Patricia Curran.

14 September 2012

Gordon died in Glasgow, aged eighty, of pneumonia and Alzheimer's disease.

Acknowledgements

I had first heard of the trial of Iain Hay Gordon in 1953, when as a Dublin eight-year-old with measles, I devoured the lengthy court reports in my father's *Irish Press*. Subsequently in a varied career in journalism, I had never found an editor whom I could convince that, given time, I could write something useful about this dreadful tale.

In 2016, I was approached by a stranger, Larry Quinn. He had read my book *The Framing of Harry Gleeson* about a man hanged for a murder committed by others. We arranged to meet in Newry, and he said he had another subject for me – Iain Hay Gordon. He talked, I listened, then I agreed.

My late brother-in-law historian Jonathan Bardon gave help and advice. Politician and author Jeff Dudgeon suggested I talk to Stratton Mills. He was a great find, hospitable and encouraging when I felt like giving up. Jim Lynn helped me greatly to understand the background to this story and dug relentlessly for further information. Joe and Heather Castles were good hosts welcoming me and giving me a conducted tour of Whiteabbey. James and Carole Turtle provided valuable evidence that I had missed.

Staff at Belfast's Linen Hall Library gave me considerable help. The Public Record Office of Northern Ireland listened patiently to my complaints about unnecessary redactions in the trial file it held and agreed to review them. Lawyers Sir Louis Blom-Cooper and John Hostettler gave valuable advice and encouragement; sadly, both have since died. Richard Graham shared his knowledge of Whiteabbey's big houses and suggested contemporary illustrations. Stephen Cameron's fascinating lecture 'Patricia Curran – A Murder Mystery' in front of a packed lunchtime audience in the Linen Hall Library in Belfast on 12 February 2018, convinced me of public interest in this case.

My thanks are also due to Bernard Adams, Ronnie and Shoshana Appleton, Rachel Armstrong, Sara Ball, Gavin Bamford, David Ian Beattie, John Bew, Conor Brady, Deaglán de Bréadún, Joe Brolly, Henry Cairns, Andrew Carnegie, Janet Carolan, Lord Carswell, Paul Clements, Emma Cowing, Hugh Crookshanks, Susan B. Cunningham, Andrew Dennis, Tariq Desai, Stephen Docherty, Ian Elliott, John and Rosemary Erskine, Godfrey Fitzsimons, Brian Garrett, Wesley Geddis, Richard Graham, Carrie Green, Keith Haine, Maud Hamill, Tom Harding, Justin Hawkins, Mark Patrick Hederman, Lady Sylvia Hermon, Jeremy Hopkin, Judith Hoben, Gwinn Hughes, Kara Hughes-Jones, Graham Joiner, Hugh Jordan, Joe Joyce, Dan Keenan, Michael Lynch, Felicity McCartney, Karen McKee, Michael McDonald, Paul McEnroe, Tim McGarry, Patsy McGuigan, Moira McMurray, Claire McNeilly, Lewis McNeice, Shirley McNeice, Nuala Macklin, Laura Maloney, Nicola Mawhinney, Christopher Moriarty, Gerry Moriarty, Joyce Murphy, Chris Mullin, Keith Nicol, Edna Nicol, Conall O'Cuinn SJ, Paul O'Kane, Patricia Radcliffe, Cathy Smith, Ian Sutherland, Jonathon Wild, Robert Wilson, Karen Wray and Trish Wylie. While these people helped me in different ways, what is written is my responsibility and mine alone.

At different stages, Duncan Webb of the *Sunday People* newspaper, John Linklater of the *Glasgow Herald* and Bruce Batten, a TV producer with BBC Northern Ireland, made significant contributions to public understanding of this miscarriage of justice, and Gordon's acquittal owes much to their work.

This book was completed with a grant from the Irish Writers Union. I thank my colleagues for their generosity and the Jonathan Williams Literary Agency for constant wholehearted support of my efforts.

Kieran Fagan, Dublin, 1 April 2022

THE ROYAL ULSTER CONSTABULARY
HEADQUARTERS, KNOCKNAGONEY HOUSE,
KNOCKNAGONEY ROAD, BELFAST NORTHERN IRELAND BT4 2PP

Telephone: (0232) 650222
Fax: (0232) 700836 Telex: (0232) 74482

Mr Henry C W Turtle
25 Bexhill Road
LONDON
SW14 7NF

Your reference:

Our reference: CM77/210/92

Date: 2*6* August 1992

Dear Sir

IAIN HAY GORDON

I am in receipt of your letter dated 16 August 1992.

Unfortunately due to the time lapse since this incident occurred, we do not hold any file at this Headquarters.

My staff have also contacted the Public Records Office at Balmoral Avenue, Belfast but again no record could be found relating to the above named and the murder you refer to.

As Mr Gordon's supervision under the Probation Service in Glasgow would be more recent, may I suggest you write to them on the matter.

Yours faithfully

J E H McIVOR
D/Chief Superintendent
for Chief Constable

Figure 13: A letter from the RUC to Henry Turtle in August 1992 saying all the files are missing! Letter courtesy James Turtle.

A note on sources

National Archives Kew, Surrey: confidential Home Office file CIM67/1/6cn Judicial Matter, Crime (NI) prerogative of mercy and pardon, possible miscarriages of Justice, Iain Hay Gordon (1953) and the Hamill Bros (1969): Confidential Northern Ireland Office file CJ3/43/100, covering same topics

Public Records Office of Northern Ireland, Titanic Quarter, Belfast: Iain Hay Gordon, file ANT/1/2/C/63/22A, and associated files.

File of documents compiled by Hugh Pierce of Justice in 1959 in support of petition for Gordon's release, including statements by Brenda and Douglas Gordon, Iain Hay Gordon, Dorothy and Henry Turtle, Dr. Desmond Curran (a psychiatrist commissioned by the Home Office) and a private detective employed by Douglas Gordon, and other items.

Linen Hall Library, Belfast and Belfast Civic Library newspaper files.

National Library of Ireland; National Photographic Archive of Ireland; National Archives of Ireland; Dublin City libraries; DLR Lexicon Library, Dun Laoghaire; Shankill Library, Co. Dublin; Antrim Town Public Library; Camden and Westminster Libraries, London; Criminal Cases Review Commission, Birmingham; Air Historical Branch of UK Ministry of Defence, Middlesex; Police Service of Northern Ireland; Friends Historical Library Dublin; Northern Ireland Courts & Tribunal Service; Holywell Hospital, Antrim; Presbyterian Historical Society of Ireland archives, Belfast; Archdiocese of Cape Town archives; Signature Group hotels, Belfast, and Northern Ireland archivist Mary Lennon's invaluable online resource www.lennonwylie.co.uk.

Select Bibliography

Joe Baker, *Old Belfast 8 –The Murder of Patricia Curran*, Belfast: Glenravel Local History Project, 2011.

Jonathan Bardon, Beyond the Studio, A history of BBC Northern Ireland, Belfast: Blackstaff Press, 2000.

John Capstick and Jack Thomas, *Given in Evidence*, London: John Long, 1960.

Susan B. Cunningham, *Sir Crawford McCullagh – Belfast's Dick Whittington*: Donaghdee, Co. Down: Laurel Cottage publishers. 2016

Jeffrey Dudgeon, *H. Montgomery Hyde*, Belfast: Belfast Press, 2018.

Gisli H. Guðjónsson, *The Psychology of Interrogations and Confessions, A Handbook*: John Wiley & Sons, 2002.

John Hostettler, *The Colour of Injustice – the mysterious murder of the daughter of a High Court judge*, Hook, Hampshire: Waterside Press, 2013.

Jean Lawrence, *The History of First United Church Dawson Creek,* Dawson Creek, British Columbia, South Peace Historical Society, undated.

Tom McAlindon, *Bloodstains in Ulster – the notorious case of Robert the Painter*, Dublin: Liffey Press, 2006.

Eoin McNamee, The Blue Tango, London: Faber & Faber, 2001.

Marc Mulholland, *To Comfort Always*, Cookstown, Co. Tyrone: Homefirst Community Trust, 1998.

Matthew Neill, *Ecclesia de Drum*, Belfast: Slieve Croob Press, 2013.

Michael Sheane, *The Story of Holywell Hospital*, Devon: Arthur H. Stockwell, 2018

Appendix 1

Iain Hay Gordon's confession to Detective Superintendent John Capstick of Scotland Yard and RUC County Inspector Albert Kennedy, 15 January 1953 at Edenmore, Whiteabbey, Co Antrim.

I left the camp at Edenmore shortly after 4 p.m. on Wednesday afternoon, the 12th of November 1952, to deliver the mail to Whiteabbey Post Office. I was in there from five to ten minutes, then went to Quiery's paper shop in the main street to collect the camp newspapers. I would not be very long in there. I believe I called in at the bookies – approximately opposite Quiery's but off the main road. I placed a bet there on a horse for one of the airmen at the camp. I forget his name. I think I then went back to the camp with the newspapers. I probably had my tea at about 5 p.m. It took me about five minutes for my tea. I think I then changed into my civilian wear of sports coat and flannels. I then walked back alone to Whiteabbey and met Patricia Curran between the Glen and Whiteabbey Post Office. She said to me, 'Hello, Iain', or something like that. I said, 'Hello, Patricia'. We had a short general conversation. I forget what we talked about, but she asked me to escort her to her home up the Glen. I agreed to do so because it was fairly dark and there was none of the family at the gate to the Glen. I can understand anyone being afraid of going up the Glen in the dark, because the light is completely cut out because the trees meet at the top. I noticed Patricia was carrying a handbag and something else – I just forget what it was. It appeared to be wrapped up whatever it was, books or something. She was wearing a yellow hat. It was just about the Glen entrance where she first spoke to me. We both walked up the Glen together and I think I was on her left-hand-side. After we had walked a few yards, I either held her left hand or arm as we walked along. She did not object and was quite cheerful. We carried on walking up the Glen until we came to the spot where the streetlamp light does not reach. It was quite dark there and I said to Patricia: 'Do you mind if I kiss you?' or words to that effect. We stopped walking and stood on the grass verge on the left-hand side of the drive. She laid her things on the grass and I think she laid her hat there as well. Before she did this, she was not keen on me giving her a kiss but consented in the end. I kissed her once or twice to begin with and she did not object. She then asked me to continue escorting her up the drive. I did not do so as I found I could not stop kissing her. As I was kissing her, I let my hand slip down her body between her coat and her clothes. Her coat was open, and my hand may have touched her breast, but I am not sure. She struggled and said: 'Don't, don't, you beast', or something like that. I struggled with her and she said to me: 'Let me go or I will tell my father.' I then lost control of myself and Patricia fell down on the grass sobbing. She appears to have fainted because she went limp. I am a bit hazy about what happened next, but I probably pulled the body of Patricia through the bushes to hide it. I dragged her by her arms or hands, but I cannot remember. Even before this happened, I do not think I was capable of knowing what I was doing. I was confused at the time and believe I stabbed her once or twice with my service knife. I had been carrying this in my trouser pocket. I am not quite sure what kind of knife it was. I may have caught her by the throat to stop her from shouting. I may have pushed her scarves against her mouth to stop her shouting. It is all very hazy to me, but I think I was disturbed, either by seeing a light or hearing footsteps in the drive. I must have remained hidden and later walked out of the Glen at the gate lodge on to the main road. As far as I know, I crossed the main road and threw the knife into the sea. I felt that something awful must have happened and quickly walked back to the camp. I went to my billet and arrived there at roughly 6.30 p.m. There was no one in the billet at that time and I saw I had some small patches of Patricia's blood on my flannels. I took a fairly large wooden nail brush from my kit. I got some water and soap from the ablutions and scrubbed the blood off my flannels. I must have done this, but I do not quite remember. As far as I know, no person saw me doing it. I then went to our central registry and did some typing as I was preparing for an examination. I went to bed at between 9.30 p.m. and 10 p.m. I got up roughly at about 7 a.m. on Thursday, the 13th of November 1952. I had my breakfast and did my routine duties. At between 8.15 a.m. and 8.30 a.m. that day, the postman was delivering mail to our camp and he told me that Mr. Justice Curran's daughter had been found dead in the grounds. He may have said she had been shot. I cannot just remember. At about 4 p.m. that day, the R.A.F. police came to the camp, checking on our movements for the previous evening. They also turned out our lockers and I saw them have a quick examination of my clothing and the contents of the lockers. On Friday, the 14th of November 1952, members of the RUC. and RAF police came to the camp. One of the RUC. men asked me where I had been during the evening of Wednesday, the 12th of November 1952. I told him I was in camp the whole of the evening from 5 p.m. I failed to tell him I had met Patricia Curran near the Glen at about 5.30 p.m. that day. Police visited our camp on a number of occasions, and I was asked to name any person who saw me in the camp after 5 p.m. on the 12th of November. I was unable to do so, and I asked about twenty people from the camp if they could, or would, say they saw me in the camp between 5 p.m. and 6 p.m. on the day of the murder. I suggested to about six or eight airmen from my billet that they should say they had seen me in the billet between 5 p.m. and 6 p.m. on Wednesday, the 12th of November 1952. I did not expect them to do this because I knew I was not there, and that they did not want to get mixed up in anything. Corporal Connor from the camp and I agreed to say that we were in the camp together and had tea; that as soon as we had finished tea, we went to the billet together. We both told this story to the RAF police although it was untrue.

I am very sorry for having killed Patricia Curran. I had no intention whatsoever of killing the girl. It was solely due to a black-out. God knows as well as anybody else that the furthest thing in my mind was to kill the girl and I ask His forgiveness. I throw myself on to the mercy of the law and I ask you to do your best for me so that I can make a complete restart in life. I should like to say how sorry I am for all the distress that I have caused the Curran family. I have felt run down for quite some time and the black-out may have been the result of over-studying and worry generally. I am also sorry for the distress and worry I have caused my dear father and mother. I ask my parents' forgiveness and if I am spared, I shall redeem my past life.

Endnotes

[i] Susan B. Cunningham, *Sir Crawford McCullagh – Belfast's Dick Whittington*, Donaghdee Co Down; Laurel Cottage publishers, 2016, p.25.

[ii] Moral Re-Armament is the way the organisation chose to spell its name. It was founded by Franck Buchman in 1938 to deepen the spirituality of Christians, and it had its origins in what was known as the Oxford Group, also led by Buchman.

[iii] *More Sinned Against than Sinning*, two one-hour TV documentaries examining the murder of Patricia Curran, BBC Northern Ireland 1995.

[iv] Tom McAlindon, *Bloodstains in Ulster*, Dublin: Liffey Press, 2006, gives a good account of this appalling case, including the jury fixing. The name of the misbehaving juryman in the first trial is revealed here on the basis of private information received in 2018.

[v] John Hostettler, *The Colour of Injustice – the mysterious murder of the daughter of a high court judge*, Eastbourne: Waterside Press, 201, pp.36-37.

[vi] Quoted in *Given in Evidence*, p.24. It is unlikely that the assistant commissioner spoke in these exact terms.

[vii] She had not been raped or strangled. Gordon probably got that information from the postman on the morning her body was found. The pathologist gave the correct version later that day, and it is odd that Gordon still hadn't got it right three days later.

[viii] Marc Mulholland *To Comfort Always,* Cookstown Co Tyrone: Homefirst Community Trust, 1998. The management committee letter has been summarised.,

[ix] Talking to Kieran Fagan on February 25, 2019, repeating sentiments expressed to Jeremy Hopkin of the *East Antrim Guardian* 20 February 2019.

[x] John Linklater *The boy who fitted the bill*, Glasgow Herald report, 11 March 1995.

[xi] Henry Brooke (1903-1984), Conservative politician and Home Secretary 1962-64; *Private Eye* magazine described him unfairly as the 'most hated man in Britain'. His family had roots in Fermanagh. A son, Peter Brooke. served as British Northern Ireland Secretary 1989-92.

[xii] Quoting an email to Kieran Fagan from Cathy Smith, 25 October 2017.

[xiii] *The History of First United Church*, Dawson Creek, British Columbia, South Peace Historical Society.

[xiv] More Sinned Against Than Sinning?, 1995 two-part TV documentary, BBC Northern Ireland. Part one was broadcast on 27 June, 1995.

[xv] Jonathan Bardon, *Beyond the Studio,* Blackstaff Press, Belfast 2000, p. 73,

[xvi] Dorothy Turtle letter to James Callaghan, 23 August 1969.

Index

Ewart, Elma 48

Faul, Revd Denis 192
Faulkner, Brian, Minister for Home Affairs 164, 189
Ferguson, James, captain of *Princess Victoria* 58
Firth, James (forensic chemist) 16, 114, 117, 121
Fitt, Gerry, MP 191
Fox, James (journalist) 147, 212